Tea for Texas

A Guide to Tearooms in the State

Lori Torrance

Republic of Texas Press

Published by Republic of Texas Press
An imprint of The Rowman & Littlefield Publishing Group, Inc.
4501 Forbes Boulevard, Suite 200
Lanham, MD 20706

Distributed by NATIONAL BOOK NETWORK

Library of Congress Cataloging-in-Publication Data

Torrance, Lori.
    Tea for Texas : a guide to tearooms in the state / by Lori Torrance.
       p. cm.
    Includes bibliographical references and index.
    ISBN 1-55622-828-7 (pbk.)
    1. Tearooms—Texas—Guidebooks. I. Title

TX907.3.T T67   2000   00-062623
647.95764—dc21   CIP

To Ginnie Bivona and the wonderful folks at the DFW Writer's Workshop for all those late nights at Denny's dispersing sage advice over the French toast,

To my sister for puppysitting during roadtrips,

To my tearoom muses: Pat, Helen, Doug, Jesse, Heather, Robin, and Mike^2,

And most especially,

To my mother; fellow tea traveler, chief navigator, photographer, and corporate worrier.

— Thanks y'all.

Contents

Contents

Contents

Contents

Contents

Contents

Contents

Introduction

The British introduced us to roses. We promptly created our own new species. They tried to lend us their dictionary, but we wrote our own. They gave us tea, but we dumped it in the harbor. They tried to share their favorite foods. We took the scones, left the kippers, and gravely pondered the shepherd's pie. Now we admit we might have been a bit hasty about the tea.

Long known in America as the "wine of the South," tea has become the second most popular drink in the states. (The first one being Tequila? Water? Dr Pepper? I'll let you guess.) Although we did manage to scandalize the Old World by dropping ice cubes in our beloved drink from time to time, there is no doubt that "we" of the New World, especially the "Texas-we," love our little flakes of pekoe.

Along with its namesake drink, tearooms have grown in popularity over the years. Once the domain of the idle elite, these special restaurants have been transformed into sanctuaries for tired antique shoppers, creative birthday party headquarters for droves of children, and the local power-lunch haunt for committees and corporate executives.

Whether you are looking for a quaint place for a bridal shower, or a welcome diversion from the fast food fodder, you will find what you seek listed here. Grab your favorite chapeau, brush up on your Emily Post, and visit the tearoom of your choice. Extended pinkies are strictly required, and violators will be forced to eat the Chocolate Decadence by themselves.

Enjoy,
Lori

"Women are like tea bags. We don't know our true strength until we are in hot water."

— Eleanor Roosevelt

West Texas/Panhandle

What is a Tearoom?

"They say they are a tearoom, but they serve barbecue for pity's sake!" Some call themselves "tearoom" and some "café," but with as many different types as there are opinions as to what one is, sometimes the line between tearoom and restaurant becomes fuzzy.

Not all tearooms serve Afternoon Tea although some restaurants and hotels do. Not all are cutesy-poo. One in particular is downright bizarre. Most serve flavored teas, but some exceptions made the cut, and the children's tearooms offer lemonade instead. Light fare generally monopolizes the menu, but smaller towns add heavier daily entrees to lure the menfolk. So, what makes a tearoom a tearoom? The following list details the qualifying features of a true tearoom for the purposes of this book. Any other point remains open for discussion.

A tearoom:

- must have a teapot within a one-mile radius of the kitchen
- does not cut your tie off at the door
- is a place you would consider taking your mother
- does not include chirpy waiters who wear expressive buttons on their suspenders
- does not have peanut shells on the floor
- has a name that does not include the words, "eats," "el," or "la"
- does not have a gas station attached to it
- does not have a dessert menu that involves a View Master
- does not have tablecloths that encourage the use of crayons
- is a tearoom because the author decided it is

1

ℳmarillo

 ## Pretend Time Tearoom

2600 Paramount, Suite C4
806-353-5319

Amarillo, the last bastion of civilization before entering the wilds of Soonerland, has long been a central meeting ground for folks braving the heat of Palo Duro Canyon, or skiers traveling to the slopes of New Mexico. One of the best places to wet the whistle in the Panhandle is at Pretend Time Tearoom, where the children can act like little adults and grownups can act like kids.

This frilly Victorian parlor in burgundy, pink florals, and lace caters to the youthful glee in all of us. The owners, Charlotte Sims, Barbara Bates, and Doris Sell, dress in maid costumes while they royally treat the birthday girl or the bride-to-be in the Princess Tea Party. Children or adults can dress in the fancy paraphernalia provided to them, including gloves, hats, fans, and even a scepter if they are feeling queenly. Sororities and shower-goers enjoy the unique service as well as ladies abandoning their husbands to the nearby golf courses, and one group consisting of five generations of women celebrated their great-great-grandmother's ninety-third birthday party.

Pretend Time serves a regular lunch in the opulent setting as well as an Afternoon Tea, a Sweet Tea that features dessert, and a Cream Tea for scone-aholics. Reservations would be a sterling idea.

House Tea: Almond Ice

Hours: Tues.-Sat. 10-5

Location: In Peppertree Square

Extended Services: Wedding and Baby Showers, Children's Dress-Up, Afternoon Tea

Ballinger

 Jeweled Sampler Tearoom

719 Hutchins
(Inside Curiosities)
915-365-5470

Pull out your polka shoes, Ballinger's annual Ethnic Festival is underway. Straddling the Atchison, Topeka, and Santa Fe Railway, Ballinger once attracted a crowd of fugitives and drifters to the saloons and gambling halls that lined Main Street. Stagecoach robberies were rampant before permanent settlers moved in and made things "civilized." Today, every spring the Ethnic Festival attracts visitors to sample Czech food, dance to German and Spanish music, and celebrate the melting pot of nationalities that merged to form Ballinger.

> "Where there's tea there's hope."
> – Sir Arthur Pinero

One of the few buildings in downtown to survive the years is the T. S. Langford Mercantile, now home to Curiosities and the Jeweled Sampler Tearoom. Iris and Alton Bryan meticulously renovated the generous expanse that once was considered for a Hilton Hotel and populated it with antique furniture, crystal, and china to fill in any gaps in your collection. Stashed among the valuables, the Jeweled Sampler offers a quiet bite to weary shoppers. The tearoom was originally owned and operated by the Bryans' daughter and still sports the tablecloths and decorations lovingly created by their daughter-in-law, Terri Bryan. The Sampler lures a special crowd devoted to its desserts, which according to the owners, will "satisfy any craving and might even start a new one."

If historic buildings intrigue you, after lunch visit the Ballinger library, built in 1909 with a Carnegie grant. After serving as an auditorium during World War II for the cadets of the Harmon Army Air Force flight school, it was renovated and placed on the National Register of Historic Places.

House Tea: Raspberry

3

Hours: (Store) Tues.-Sat. 9:30-5; (Lunch) Tues.-Sat. 11-2

Location: Hutchins is also Highway 67

Extended Services: Wedding and Baby Showers, Rehearsal Dinners, Catering

Borger

 Grand Street Tearoom

100 W. Grand
(Inside the House of Coffee)
806-274-9404

Grand Street is a tearoom in its truest sense; it only opens on days that start with the letter "T." Consider rearranging your calendar to pencil in lunch at this unusual ten-table bistro. The food and atmosphere make the trip well worth the effort. Located in the rear of a renovated 1926 hotel, Grand Street shares its floor with a coffee bar and a gift shop. The upper windows of the multistory brick reveal the history of the building from hotel to pharmacy to doctor's office in painted vignettes facing the streets.

Inside, the dark paneling, forest green accents, and Chandolien lamps give this tearoom an English pub feel. The bronze scales, mirrors, and clocks used in decoration are mostly antiques and are all for sale. The menu changes at the artistic whim of owner René Brain, who enjoys delighting Panhandle natives with recipes from *Southern Living* cookbooks. Entrees might include chicken pecan quiche, Caribbean shrimp and black bean salad, or jalapeño stuffed pork loin to keep things interesting.

While you wait for your table, pick up the *Grand Street Tea Times* newsletter written by René. Upcoming events, such as the "Texas Comes to the Tearoom" cookout, are posted along with special recipes of the month.

House Tea: Almond Mocha

Hours: Tues., Thurs. 11-2

Location: Corner of Main and Grand

Extended Services: Wedding and Baby Showers, Rehearsal Dinners, Children's Dress-Up, Coffee Bar

El Paso

 ## The Mad Hatter

7933 North Mesa, Suite H
915-845-1800

"Pardon me, but have you seen a rather large white rabbit?" Doubtlessly, he is having tea at the Mad Hatter. Inspired by the owner's love of the C. S. Lewis classic; the name, the menu, and the decorations reflect the tea party scene from *Alice in Wonderland*. As you walk in the front door of the gift shop, the owner's personal collection of *Alice* memorabilia catches the eye first, but not for long. The store with the Department 56 houses, the Televara pottery, and the Coutour of New York handbags overwhelms the shopping senses. Everywhere you look, collection completers cry out to you to buy them. Patricia Sprat linens and southwest fashion clothing lie calmly next to the

"Take some more tea," the March Hare said to Alice, very earnestly.

"I've had nothing yet," Alice replied in an offended tone, "so I can't take more."

"You mean, you can't take _less_," said the Hatter: "It's very easy to take more than nothing."

– Lewis Carroll

antique colonial furniture and Elsie Massey dolls.

Don't forget to save some money for lunch. This haven of Yankee snowbirds serves its repast on vintage china with estate silver. The room is mellow in southwest pastels with teal carpet and dusty rose tablecloths, and each of the tables sports an antique salt and pepper set. From the menu, try the White Rabbit Salad with ten different greens, or choose any of the other dishes named for characters in the book. Fortunately, the Mad Hatter stays open later than most tearooms, so you still have time to shop after lunch.

House Tea: Raspberry and Apricot

Hours: Tues.-Sat. 10-7, Sun. 10-5

Location: Doniphan Street and North Mesa on the far west side of El Paso

Extended Services: Wedding and Baby Showers, Rehearsal Dinners, Catering

Window Box

4727 Hondo Pass, Suite F
915-751-4355

For most Texans, El Paso seems generally regarded as the last civilized watering hole before the Sahara of the Southwest. Located at the end of

6

the Texas tire-eater Interstate-10, El Paso serves as a jumping-off point for the snowy dunes of White Sands, the bat resort of Carlsbad Caverns, and the alien theme park of Roswell. To the south, Ciudad Juarez lies across the Rio Grande. Each year thousands of tourists and a large number of prom-night teenagers cross the bridge by car or on foot, seeking adventure or at least a good margarita. One word of warning: Crossing the toll bridge may not be the best time to do your Jay Leno impression. Border guards are not known for their vivacious sense of humor. For a true insight into the job, spend a couple of fascinating hours at the Border Patrol Museum on the U.S. side. The display of confiscated items will give you the best laugh of the day.

Just because you are in El Paso does not mean you have to eat Mexican food. The Window Box on the northeast side offers a welcome respite from the daily tamale. Fountains bubble in the corner of this terrace garden tearoom. Patio furniture in summery green stripes and window boxes full of flowers radiate an outdoor serenity without the mosquitoes. Window Box also provides Teddy Bear Dress-Up parties for children of whatever age. Participants can invite the grizzly of their choice, dressed in finery or bear-bottomed. The house teddy-in-charge presides over the table of bear-shaped cakes and sandwiches. The *pièce de résistance* is, of course, Teddigram cookies.

> "Love and scandal are the best sweeteners of tea."
>
> – Henry Fielding

While you are digesting, drive the scenic Trans-Mountain Road (Loop 375) through the mountains. Yes, Virginia, Texas does have mountains, and not just in "X-Files" movies. The 360-degree view of the surrounding states and both countries is breathtaking if your car can manage the incline. For your blood pressure sake, don't try this road with a trailer or faulty brakes.

House Tea: Black Cherry, Amaretto, or Raspberry in rotation

Hours: (Continental Breakfast) Tues.-Sat. 9:30-11; (Lunch) Tues.-Sat. 11-4

Location: Northeast El Paso, near Dyer

Extended Services: Wedding and Baby Showers, Rehearsal Dinners, Catering, Children's Dress-Up (Saturdays from 3-4)

Lubbock

 ## The English Garden

6409 Indiana Avenue
(Inside KK's Craft Mall)
806-799-8322

If you are driving through the desert and see a tall man with a lance astride a horse, followed by a short man on a mule, you are either near L.A. or the New American Wind-Powered Center in Lubbock. Featuring twenty-eight acres of windmills, one of the world's largest collections, Señor Quixote will really have an impossible dream. Inside the center, hundreds of these nineteenth-century, oversized pinwheels reach the roof. Historically fascinating even for an internal-combustion kind of person, they rekindle a fond romance for the prairie, a sunset, and a lone whirligig squeaking in the breeze.

When you finish, propel yourself to the English Garden Tearoom for some Sante Fe soup and ambrosia cake. Located in KK's Craft Mall, the double handful of floral tables and wooden chairs inside the white picket fence gather under the twinkling lights and ivy-covered ceiling. Owned by "Madame President" Rae Capogna, the tearoom employs her son Chad for the hours that extend from breakfast to dinner. When the craft mall closes, Rae invites her guests to enter through the tearoom's back door, like neighbors. Instead of borrowing a cup of coffee, though, you can have yours here along with a generous slab of spice cake.

House Tea: Peach, Lemon Zinger, and Cinnamon Apple

Hours: (Store) Mon.-Sat. 9-9, Sun. 1-6; (Lunch) Mon.-Sat. 9-8, Sun. 11-5

Location: 66th and Indiana

Extended Services: Wedding and Baby Showers, Rehearsal Dinners, Children's Dress-Up, Afternoon Tea

The Rose Teapot

3121 34th Street

806-792-0075

I cannot tell a lie; George Washington and his wife frequent the Rose Teapot when they are visiting Lubbock. To further the historical education of local children, the Rose Teapot and the local elementary schools sponsor a special Tea with the President. The children dress in colonial clothing and watch as the man who is "first in war, first in peace, and first in the hearts of his countrymen" gallops up to the plate glass window on his stallion, dismounts, and regales the eager students with tales of Valley Forge and crossing the Delaware. Joining him is his faithful wife, Martha; Ben Franklin, sans the kite; and John Paul "I have not yet begun to fight" Jones. Each gets a chance to captivate their audience with stories of a bygone age. The horse takes his tea in the great outdoors.

> "We had a kettle; we let it leak:
> Our not repairing made it worse.
> We haven't had any tea for a week...
> The bottom is out of the Universe."
>
> – Rudyard Kipling

Many church groups and bridge players also make the Rose Teapot their home away from home. Two of the mauve and green rooms are set aside for the twelve permanent bridge groups that meet there. For the local churches that frown on cards, this tearoom is also the main spot for forty-two, the Baptist answer to spades. The two-tiered antique and gift mall and the English garden-themed tearoom are truly family owned. Four generations of women run the 15,000-square-foot mall and its small dining area with the antique chairs and lace table runners. If you visit, consider making reservations. George draws a big crowd.

House Tea: Raspberry

Hours: (Store) Mon.-Sat. 10-6; (Lunch) Mon.-Fri. 11-2, Sat. 11-3, desserts until 6 P.M.

Location: 34th and Flint

Extended Services: Wedding and Baby Showers, Rehearsal Dinners, Children's Dress-Up

Plainview

 Season's Way

2900 Olton Road #7

806-291-0777

Nestled between Amarillo and Lubbock lies Plainview, named for its magnificent view of the plains. Sitting on the only shallow underground water belt for miles, the home of Jimmy Dean sausage has emerged as a cozy little community with great shopping and a one-of-a-kind tearoom.

As you walk up the brick-painted stairs from the ground floor flower shop, the building begins to resemble the great outdoors. The painted floors appear as patio tiles, and along with the earthy colors and silk flowers, the diners feel like they are eating on an upscale terrace. Of special interest on the menu are the hearty soups served in sourdough bread bowls *à la* San Francisco, and the blackberry cobbler, the stuff of dream cravings. On your way out, don't forget to buy yourself a present at the lingerie boutique. They carry all the favorites, including Katherine's.

House Tea: Raspberry

Hours: (Store) Mon.-Fri. 10-5; (Lunch) Mon.-Fri. 11:30-1:30

Location: Olton is also Fifth Street

Extended Services: Wedding and Baby Showers, Rehearsal Dinners, Children's Dress-Up

> "Tea leaves are richer than most fruits
> and vegetables in antioxidant
> compounds."
>   – Newsweek Magazine, October 1998

Hill Country

How to Make a Perfect Cup of Tea

The Proper Epicurean Cup of Tea

1. Place cold, filtered water in a teakettle.
2. Bring to a full boil, but remove before it comes to a rolling boil. Overboiling will flatten the taste.
3. Pour one cup into a clay teapot. (A Brown Betty teapot is best.)
4. Swish it around and then pour it out. This will heat the pot properly.
5. Place loose tea in the pot (½-1 teaspoon for each cup to be made). If more than 6 cups, add a teaspoon "for the pot."
6. Place boiled water in the pot.
7. Pour a little of the water off to "rinse the tea leaves."
8. Infuse exactly 3 minutes. (For green tea, infuse for 1½-2½ minutes with the lid off.)
9. Shake the pot to let the leaves settle.
10. Decant the tea into a second warmed pot (a serving teapot). If the tea is a two-water tea, it can be used a second time. But never drink tea that is left overnight; it has adverse physical effects.
11. Rinse the cups with hot water.
12. Pour milk in the cup if desired. Milk added before the tea will keep porcelain from cracking. Never use cream; it curdles.
13. Add sugar if desired.
14. Add tea.
15. Cover serving pot with a tea cozy.

The Not-So-Proper-But-Still-Acceptable Cup of Tea

1. Let the cold tap run for a while, then fill the teakettle.
2. Boil water until it sprays the wall behind your stove.
3. Pour one cup into a clay teapot.
4. Swish it around and then pour it out. This will heat the pot properly.
5. Place loose tea in the pot (½-1 teaspoon for each cup to be made).
6. Place boiled water in the pot.
7. Brew for 3-5 minutes. Use less time for less caffeine. Don't brew longer to get a darker tea; add more tea leaves instead.
8. Decant the tea into a second pot (a serving teapot). The new designer pots have lead glazes. Don't use teapots that are only for show or you might go the way of the Roman Empire.

An Eminently More Practical Cup of Tea

1. Place cold tap water in a teakettle.
2. Boil water until the whistle reminds you that you left the kettle on.
3. Place loose tea in a teapot (1 teaspoon for each cup to be made).
4. Place boiled water in the teapot.
5. Brew until you have dug out the year-old Girl Scout cookies hiding in the back of your freezer under the permafrost.
6. Strain the tea into a cup.

A Cup of Tea for the Modern Age

1. Nuke cold tap water in the microwave on the popcorn setting.
2. Throw a tea bag in a cup.
3. Remove the tea bag when bottom of spoon in cup is no longer visible.
4. Throw the tea bag in old mug on counter to be used for next month's facial.

Austin

 ## Momoko Bubble Tea and Japanese Gifts

705A West 24th Street
512-469-0232

Austin, home of the artsy and clever, is the perfect place for Momoko, a celebration of tea Japanese style. With none of the Victorian trappings that Americans have come to expect in a tearoom, Momoko is more like a tea bar. The owner, We-linning Ko, acts as bartender, mixing combinations of tea for the diverse crowd that frequents the shop. Visitors can request their own special blend without the obligation of paying for it if their concoction was ill chosen. Better yet, let the proprietress select something that you will like.

For twenty years, she watched her father mixing teas in Taiwan. Even though the leaves are mostly from Japan, the idea of mixing teas is a part of a long Taiwanese history. Now, We-linning spends most of her time introducing the craft to grateful Austinites. As she so aptly says on her business cards, "If I am not at home, I am at Momoko. If I am not at Momoko, I am on my way to Momoko."

The mixtures fall into the categories of blended, herbal, fruit, natural flavor, milk, and health. The combination of the brewed leaves and shaken ingredients produces hundreds of tastes. Some are designed for health, some for people who don't like the taste of tea. Some leaves don't go on the menu for months, while the owner decides how best to mix them. Some unusual choices include tart Granny Apple, Chocolate Tea made with cocoa, Mallow Blue for clearing the voice and vision, Chiyedun to lower cholesterol and high blood pressure, and Coffee Milk tea, because it tastes great. If you are hungry, try a sushi or rice ball. They come in both vegetarian and carnivorous. Incidentally, Momoko means "peach child" in Japanese. Peach is the symbol of good luck.

House Tea: Hundreds to choose from

Hours: Mon.-Thurs. 11-8, Fri.-Sat. 11-10, Sun. 12-8

Location: Just off campus

Extended Services: Catering

 ## Wilson's Texas Tearoom

12703 W. Highway 71
512-263-1950

In any other hot and humid city you'd be the carnivore du jour at the mosquito smorgasbord, but not in Austin, bat capital of Texas. Those vampire-wanna-bes, who are actually cute in a Ewok/troll doll sort of way, pick their teeth nightly after a six-course wing fling. At sunset you can watch them all rush for takeout at the same time, like halftime during the Superbowl. Most of the year, the bats hang out at their fashionable lakefront villa, the Town Lake bridge. But every winter they hop in their batmobiles and make a run for the border, where they eat lots of spicy insects, drink tequila, and come back with tattoos. All of which has absolutely nothing to do with Wilson's Texas Tearoom, which does not serve mosquitoes, spicy or otherwise, but does serve an excellent lunch, brunch, and Afternoon Tea.

Stashed in the corner of Wilson's Fine Furniture, the double handful of refined tables make themselves at home among the leopard print pillows, ceramic giraffes, and upscale furniture. The tearoom specializes in Afternoon Tea, which is reputedly the best of the area, but also offers a gourmet lunch menu with items named after Texas bodies of water.

"Tea pot is on, the cups are waiting,
Favorite chairs anticipating,
No matter what I have to do,
My friend there's always time for you."

– Anonymous

The Barton Creek salad features field greens with chicken, pine nuts, and Gorgonzola cheese served as icy as its namesake. The Lake Austin Caesar salad comes with blackened salmon, and the Town Lake Greek salad was probably inspired by the wild bat ouzo parties under the bridge.

Wilson's plans to move this year to a new building on Route 2244 from their current home at Bee Caves Road. The new location promises a larger dining area to accommodate the increased demand of Austin visitors.

House Tea: Twenty varieties

Hours: Tues.-Sun. 11-2:30

Location: Just west of Bee Caves Road

Extended Services: Wedding and Baby Showers, Rehearsal Dinners, Receptions, Afternoon Tea, Sunday Brunch

Menu

Salads

Brazos - Grilled chicken breast on field greens with tomato, sprouts, egg, bacon bits, and cheese with balsamic vinaigrette or honey mustard

Town Lake - Greens, Romaine lettuce, green onion, olives, tomato, sprouts, feta cheese, and boiled egg, tossed in a balsamic feta vinaigrette

Lake Austin - Crisp Romaine lettuce, Parmesan cheese, and house Caesar dressing, topped with garlic croutons

Inks Lake - Chinese vegetables and sliced chicken breast tossed in plum ginger sesame dressing

Barton Creek - Field greens tossed in a honey garlic dressing, topped with chicken, roasted red bell pepper, corn, pine nuts, and Gorgonzola cheese

Trinity - Shredded chicken breast with garlic, herbs, carrot, celery, and onion in a light dressing

Sandwiches

Pedernales - Marinated grilled chicken breast with melted Jack cheese, salsa presilla, field greens, and roasted red bell peppers on focaccia bread

Sabine - Chicken salad, ham, or turkey piled on wheat sourdough or focaccia bread

Comal - Chicken salad, tomato, avocado, bacon, and ranch dressing on seven-grain bread

Rio Grande - Grilled chicken, tomato, avocado, and melted Jack cheese on sourdough bread

Blanco - Turkey, sauerkraut, Swiss cheese, and Russian dressing piled on toasted seven-grain bread

Lake LBJ - Breast of chicken, lettuce, tomato, and onion with salsa presilla and spicy chipotle sauce on sourdough

Burnet

 ## Gloria's Dream Cottage

301 E. League
512-756-0277

Rumble through the rustic terrain on one of the few active steam locomotives in America, as the *Hill Country Flyer* transports you from Austin to Burnet and back in time. In Burnet (that's Burn-it, dern-it, when ya' gonna learn it) you can do what folks of the Old West did: arrive in town by train, shop, have some lunch, shop, gawk at the dancehall girls, shop, watch men get shot during a poker fight, and jump on the train and get "out of Dodge."

While you are there, be sure to visit Gloria's Dream Cottage, a restored Victorian house that caters outdoor teas and other large functions, such as weddings, during the milder Texas months. The two tables inside are seasonally unavailable for tea depending on the inventory. Once you visit, you'll understand why. The cottage is filled inside and out with an eyeful of collectibles. Concrete rabbits burrow through the ivy in the front yard. Real cats play jungle-kitty among the flowers and metal sculptures. China plates line the walkways. The cottage is especially appealing when adorned in all its Christmas splendor.

On your way out, if you see a plate buried in the garden that is particularly appealing, feel free to purchase it and take it home for your very own. Gloria says that people buy the dishware right out of the ground.

House Tea: N/A

Hours: (Store) Tues.-Sat. 10-5, outdoor functions by reservation only

Location: Behind the main square

Extended Services: (Outdoor facilities only) Weddings, Receptions, Private Parties

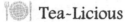 Tea-Licious

216 S. Main
512-756-7636
http://www.tealicious.com

When Vickie and Sam McLeod moved from Houston to Burnet, they didn't plan on opening a tearoom. Burnet was a relatively sleepy town at that time with some very nice ranching acreage, which drew them up there. Vickie entertained the notion of creating a place for people to meet for lunch. At first Sam was unsure as to the longevity of a tearoom in a town of 3,400, but he renovated a 1,500-square-foot building downtown for the new site. Much to their delight, the tearoom became the main "let's do lunch" place in town. In fact, the volume increased so rapidly that Sam quit his medical business to help run the restaurant. When the vintage Ford dealership building became available, Sam restored it, and Tea-Licious moved to the larger building.

Tea-Licious is bright and airy with a painted picket fence on the front facade. The tin roof and rock walls are authentic, and the clean country interior was decorated by Vickie. The colorful quilts covering the walls are for sale, but were originally hung to dampen the acoustics in the building. On the right side of the restaurant is a gift shop that sells fun gifts and wraps in quite a variety, including teapot sneaker charms and jars of homemade pickles. The pickles are a specialty of the house and are a "must taste." The recipe came from a buddy of Sam's, who revealed his grandmother's secret concoction on a long hunting trip years ago. After years of recipe refinement, they are now sold nationally.

> "The cozy fire is bright and gay,
> The merry kettle boils away
> And hums a cheerful song.
> I sing the saucer and the cup;
> Pray, Mary, fill the teapot up,
> And do not make it strong."
>
> – Barry Pain

Last year, Tea-Licious began sponsoring an upscale block party. With the help of the Chambers of Commerce from Burnet and the surrounding towns, they close the main street down in front of the tearoom for an evening of frolic with finesse. Circular tables are brought out with fresh linen and fine champagne flutes. While the band plays jazz and Motown, the diners partake of filet mignon and other delicacies prepared by Tea-Licious and dance on the paved dance floor created just for the occasion. The affair has been so successful that now it is held biannually. So, now you can do your Diana Ross impression twice a year.

House Tea: Peach

Hours: Mon.-Sat. 11-3

Location: On the main square

Extended Services: Wedding and Baby Showers, Rehearsal Dinners, Receptions, Catering, Tour Companies

Menu

Salads

Garden Salad - Green leaf lettuce, tomato, bell pepper, cucumber, purple onion, house dressing, croutons, and cheese

Chicken or Tuna Salad - Served on lettuce with choice of chips, potato salad, or fruit

Special Garden Salad - Green leaf lettuce, tomato, bell pepper, cucumber, purple onion, house dressing, croutons, cheese, and chicken or tuna salad

Sandwiches

Chicken Salad Delight - Chicken breast with capers and house mayo

Spinach Garden Wrap - Guacamole, cucumber, mushrooms, tomato, and cheese on spinach leaf

Cheesy Pimento Cheese - A blend of cheeses and pimento with a hint of sugar

Tuna-Licious - Chunk light tuna with pecans and sweet pickle relish

Smoked Turkey - Smoked turkey breast served with Dijon mustard, lettuce, tomato, and Swiss cheese

Entrees

Monday = French Dip - Roast beef on French loaf served with au jus sauce

Tuesday = Beef Cheddar Melt - Roast beef with melted cheese and horseradish sauce on an onion roll

Wednesday = Reuben - Corned beef with Dijon mustard on grilled rye

Thursday = Beef Fajita Wrap - Mesquite grilled beef in herbal wrap with melted cheese and sautéed onion, guacamole, and ranch sour cream

Friday = Special Garden Salad - Leaf lettuce, tomato, bell pepper, cucumber, purple onion, house dressing, croutons, cheese, and chicken or tuna salad

Saturday = Smoked Turkey - Smoked turkey breast with Dijon mustard, lettuce, tomato, and Swiss cheese

Comfort

 Arlenne's Country Café

426 7th Street
830-995-3330

Don't let the pig sign in the front yard fool you; the closest thing to barbe-cue Arlenne's serves is French ham salad on sourdough. Called a "country café" to prevent the local men from getting ABS brake lockup when enter-ing the front door, the oleo yellow Victorian house is the home and semiretirement project of *San Antonio Express* columnist Arlenne Lightsey.

When Arlenne was growing up, her mother cooked all the meals for their huge family and the extra Sunday-go-to-church guests. Arlenne got to wash the dishes. Since her mother had a tendency to use every dish in the house when she cooked, the daughter made her parent an offer she couldn't refuse, they'd trade places. This turned out to be a golden deal for Mama since Arlenne cleaned as she cooked. Today, the mistress of the house still sets extra places on Sunday, their busiest day.

Locals visit the café with the subdued tearoom decor for the yeast bis-cuits with molasses butter and the daily specials that made their way into the restaurant's cookbook. The desserts stored under glass in the

21

entryway are Arlenne's special love and include plenty of old-fashioned favorites, like a butter cake with orange buttercream frosting, and Sawdust Pie with coconut, bananas, and graham crackers. Beware the Utterly Deadly Pecan Pie. This dentist's dream dessert is the original comfort food.

House Tea: Raspberry

Hours: Thurs.-Sun. 11-4

Location: Downtown

Extended Services: Wedding and Baby Showers, Catering, Afternoon Tea

 ## Summer House Tearoom

105 Highway 473
(Inside the Haven River Inn)
830-995-3834
http://www.bed-breakfast-comfort.com

"Mumsy, mumsy, let's go down to the summer house for tea." If you never bothered to build a second home, try the one at the Haven River Inn. The twenty-three acres sprawling on the Guadalupe River once belonged to a San Antonio lumber tycoon in the early 1900s as his getaway spot during the warmer months. Now the stately home and acreage have found a new life as a bed and breakfast and golf course.

Downstairs, Barbara Pankratz and Julie Heinen present Afternoon Tea in the refined rose and hunter green dining area and enclosed porch. Lace-draped tables bear pink and green Depression-era cups, saucers, and sherbet dishes used for the multicourse delicacies. The matching gold, pink, and green floral china comes from Barbara's private collection of many years.

Each diner may choose from several menus that rotate monthly, including a Cream Tea, a Light Afternoon Tea, and a Full Afternoon Tea sampler for the very hungry. Each menu includes an appetizer drink, like White Grape-Peach, cheese straws, and a choice of tea, including Eastern Shore's appropriately named Summer House Tea. One month the scone might be maple-oatmeal, and the savory, a choice of sausage roll or petite quiche. Finger sandwiches, sweets, and cake varieties change with the menu, and the Work of Art cookies rotate with the season. These almond cookies with their colorful icing are the natural result of Barbara's massive cookie cutter collection. Special parties can request certain shapes as befits the occasion from literally hundreds of choices. For a novel party, ask about Summer House's tea tastings and etiquette classes.

House Tea: Summer House Tea

Hours: Thurs. 3-5

Location: Highway 473 at I-10

Extended Services: Wedding and Baby Showers, Catering, Afternoon Tea

Fredericksburg

 Fredericksburg Herb Farm

403 Whitney Street
830-997-8615
http://www.fredericksburgherbfarm.com

A hawk circles lazily overhead, and the summer sounds of birds and cicadas float across the flowering fields of the Fredericksburg Herb Farm. Situated on fourteen acres that was both a pioneer home and the cannery for World War II victory gardens, the collection of historic buildings, gardens, creeks, and greenhouses create a compelling haven unlike any other. On the far end of the property, a star-shaped garden centers around a windmill. The sweet-smelling herbs grown there appear in the food at the tearoom, and in the oils, soaps, and vinegar sold at the main house. Next to the working garden that provides the lettuce, onions, and other essentials to a happy bunny diet, the Poet's House sells gardening gifts, books, and fragrant candles for every fussy nose. The Quiet Haus offers aromatherapy, massages, and facials using, of course, their own lotions and oils.

Among the cool stone walls of the main house lies the tearoom and apothecary. Dried flowers hang from the rafters over the bottles of creams and lotions made in every flavor imaginable. Down the stone stairs, the tearoom extends through the sunroom, greenhouse, and adjoining corridors. The solarium is composed entirely of windows and ceiling beams. Bright and crispy clean, this room remains the favorite spot for large parties. Two-tops dot the corridors and greenhouse room and spill onto the gravel patio, where umbrellas protect diners from the Hill Country rays. Wooden swings overlook the garden next door.

The Herb Farm Tearoom makes all of its gourmet restaurant-style food from their own gardens and often decorate the plates with edible flowers. The dessert menu is ingenious and has its own following as does the Good Thyme Sangria, the beverage of choice for hot summer afternoons.

If you don't want to leave, make reservations at the Herb Haus Bed and Breakfast next to the main building. It will baby you with footed tubs, herbal toiletries, and a continental breakfast featuring homemade bread and handmade jellies. You may want to move in permanently.

House Tea: Harvest Herb Tea

Hours: (Store) Mon.-Sat. 9:30-5:30, Sun. 1-4; (Lunch) Tues.-Sat. 11-3

Location: Main Street to Milam, six blocks south

Extended Services: Wedding and Baby Showers, Rehearsal Dinners, Receptions, Bed and Breakfast, Day Spa, Herb Farm

Menu

Salads

The Working Herb Garden - Spring greens, pear tomato, onion, cucumber, and celery with Hill Country blueberry vinaigrette

Caesar Salad - With roasted basil tomato, croutons, and Parmesan cheese

Sylvia's Bouquet Dill Chicken Salad - With toasted pecans, black olives, green onion, and chunky pineapple in a dilly dip

Broiled Peach Salad - With baby spinach and herb feta in a champagne vinaigrette

Sandwiches

Balsamic Marinated Portobella Sandwich - With Roma tomato and mozzarella on European sourdough with basil pesto

Black Buck Antelope Burger - Layered with Monterey Jack, field greens, roasted tomato, and smoky chili mayonnaise on a round bun

Entrees

Ricotta Stuffed Tortellini - With sautéed Gulf shrimp in a garlic and parsley white wine broth

Oven Roasted Chicken Fajita Wrap - With avocado, pepper, onion, tomato, mixed greens, and Jack cheese on a mild chipotle tortilla

The Peach Tree

210 South Adams
830-997-9527

The Mecca of all tearooms lies in Fredericksburg, the bed and breakfast capital of Texas. Named after the acres of telltale orchards surrounding this German city, the Peach Tree attracts tea pilgrims worldwide to sample the cuisine lauded by *Gourmet Magazine*, *The Dallas Morning News*, and the *San Antonio Express-News*. After three best-selling cookbooks, it is hard to say whether the tearoom made the cookbooks famous or vice versa.

Inside the crowded house, the glazed terra-cotta tiles lead you through rooms filled with a browser's delight of gifts and eventually to the sunny alcove rooms wrapped around a garden atrium. Peach Tree's fame arises not from frilly accouterments, but from the gourmet cuisine that changes daily and is served ever so artistically. The house tea is, of course, Peach served with a lime wedge in a hefty tumbler. Fresh bread, including jalapeño cheese, sun-dried tomato pesto with walnuts, and Asiago cheese with spiced pepitas, comes with the entrees or can be purchased in the gift shop deli with the other specialties of the house. The simple menu might include chilled avocado soup decorated with a little heart drawn in sour cream, or chicken vegetable liberally supplied with crushed peppercorns, but all are equally excellent including the desserts made with Ghirardelli chocolate.

If you plan to pilgrimage anytime soon, reservations may be your best idea of the month. From noon to two, this Grand Central Station of tea-rooms stays booked.

House Tea: Peach, of course

Hours: (Store) Mon.-Sat. 9:30-5:30; (Lunch) Mon.-Sat. 11-2:30

Location: Off Main Street

Extended Services: Wedding and Baby Showers, Rehearsal Dinners, Catering, Gourmet Takeout

Menu

Salads

Cynthia's Chicken Salad - Made with chunks of chicken, an herbal mayonnaise, green onion, celery, and capers

Ensalada Veracruz - A large Mexican salad of leafy gourmet lettuce, black beans, guacamole, Monterey Jack cheese, tomato, tortilla chips, and house dressing or lime-cilantro fat-free dressing

Caesar Salad - Cold, crisp Romaine lettuce tossed with a Caesar dressing and topped with grated Asiago cheese and herbed croutons

Greek Salad - A large green salad with feta cheese, Greek olives, pepperocini pepper, tomato, red onion, cucumber, and a dressing made with Greek oregano, garlic, and red wine

Sandwiches

Cynthia's Chicken Salad - Made with chunks of chicken breast, herbal mayonnaise, green onion, celery, and Mediterranean capers

Tuna Salad - White Albacore tuna with herbal mayonnaise, walnuts, green onion, celery, and sprouts

Jalapeño-Pimento Cheese - Grated cheddar and Monterey Jack cheeses, jalapeño, pimento, mayonnaise, and lettuce

Turkey Pocket Croissant - Pocket croissant filled with smoked turkey breast, Muenster cheese, lettuce, tomato, red onion, and herbal mayonnaise

Veggie Sandwich - Herbal mayonnaise with sliced olives, lettuce, tomato, sprouts, mushrooms, cucumber, avocado, and cream cheese

Croissant Sandwich - A crusty croissant layered with peppered ham, Muenster cheese, sprouts, black olives, cucumber, and herb mayonnaise

Marble Falls

Mim's Whim

617 Broadway
830-693-8976

While living in Australia and daily frequenting the very busy tearooms down under, "Mim," as she was called by her grandchildren, dreamed of one day owning a tearoom. For years she collected china and glassware for that special dream-to-be. Years later the owner of Mim's and More B&B and Tearoom has had her dream realized not once, but twice. The 100-year-old house that now is the home of the bed and breakfast and Mim's Whim Tearoom is actually the second location to bear that name.

Originally, Mim's and More Bed and Breakfast resided across town. The current house, found by a friend just over a year ago, was originally unfinished upstairs. The bedrooms on the top floor now serve as a bed and breakfast. Downstairs, the sunny patio tearoom with its expanse of windows and antique chandeliers is the favorite choice for sorority dinners and other local engagements. In the evenings, the white lights in the ficus trees give the room an intimate glow.

> "Look here, Steward, if this is coffee, I want tea; but if this is tea, then I wish for coffee."
>
> – Punch

Evidence of the owner's former occupation, fashion merchandising, lends ambiance to the downstairs rooms. Pristine vintage hats dot the front room. They are worn during children's tea parties, the birthday girl naturally getting first dibs. During wedding showers, antique wedding gowns provide the appropriate decorative flair. In the parlor, several racks of hand selected artsy clothing are available for sale. So, you can go into tea adorned in your new finery.

House Tea: Rotates daily

Hours: (Store) Tues.-Fri. 10-4, Sat. 10-3; (Lunch) Tues.-Sat. 11-2:30

Location: Just past the intersection of 281 and 1431

Extended Services: Wedding and Baby showers, Rehearsal Dinners, Receptions, Children's Dress-Up, Bed and Breakfast

Menu

Salads

The Garden Salad - Mixed leaf greens, tomato, cucumber, carrot, and hard-boiled eggs

Sandwiches

Chicken Salad	Reuben
Ham and Cheese	Turkey and Cheese

Hearty Grilled Cheese on Sourdough
Mim's Spicy Pimento Cheese on Raisin Toast

Entrees

Quiche	Shrimp Cocktail

Round Rock

 J'Anna Rose

1601 S. IH 35
(Inside the Round Rock Antique Mall)
512-310-7878

"Come back to a time when there was rest for the spirit and sweetness for the soul." The lovely motto of the J'Anna Rose reflects the harmonious simplicity of the Round Rock Antique Mall's tearoom. Owner Jane Voigt employs her extensive interior design background to create a peaceful hideaway for shoppers to rest and refuel. Black chairs, shutters, and vintage accents set off the sage walls and cream striped tables. Shabby chic crackle-wood doors serve as room dividers, and Ascot hats in black and cream dot the walls and perch on the sage mantel. The decor, like the menu, changes on the whim of the owner, whose culinary experiments have won competitions all over the state.

The menu revolves around the excellent soups served both hot and chilled. The creamy chicken avocado, their signature dish, was created for the Golden Kiss Chicken Contest, which it won. Don't overlook the cold cucumber soup, ginger Oriental chicken noodle, or the chilled strawberry soup, which sounds odd if you haven't had it, but is fabulous for hot summer days.

Speaking of summer, the Round Rock Express has a new home right down the road. The recently formed AA professional baseball team will be playing all season at the Dell Express Stadium, compliments of Round Rock's biggest employer, Dell Computer. Don't forget the Cracker Jacks.

House Tea: Raspberry, Peach, and Hot Ginger Peach

Hours: (Store) Mon.-Sun. 10-7; (Lunch) Tues.-Sat. 11:30-2:30

Location: Exit 251 off I-35

Extended Services: Wedding and Baby Showers, Rehearsal Dinners, Afternoon Tea

> "If you are cold, tea will warm you;
> If you are too heated, it will cool you;
> If you are depressed, it will cheer you;
> If you are excited, it will calm you."
>
> – Gladstone

North Central

Tasseography - It's in the Leaves

Astound your friends and fellow scone munchers; read their tea leaves and predict your next tea party. This ancient art of divination requires a hefty dose of imagination from the diviner, but a firm grasp of human character helps a great deal.

Start by brewing a pot of tea. Large-leaf tea will be easier to read than the "dust" of industrial teas, but either works better than a tea bag, in which the future may appear a bit blank. Pour the unstrained tea into a wide cup and ask the seeker to drink it until only a bare teaspoon of liquid remains. Remember, if he or she drinks any of the leaves in the process, they are effectively swallowing their future. Rotate the cup three times counterclockwise with your left hand. Turn the cup upside down into a saucer and rotate it three times counterclockwise again with your left hand. The presence of the saucer bears no significance to the reading, only to your carpet. Have your victim turn the cup so that the handle faces you. This extends the person's aura into the cup, so the leaves won't get confused and predict the future of someone at the table behind you. When you flip the cup over, the leaf carcasses should be spread around enough for a proper reading.

To the untrained eye, they may appear as little piles of soggy detritus, but to a practiced cloud watcher or advertising executive, you could be looking at a frog on a bicycle. Ah, a Muppets movie is in your future. To determine when and where you'll catch this flick, analyze the position of the leaves. If Kermit peddles near the rim, then you may be making a late run to the video store tonight. If he cycles at the bottom, you may catch it in reruns next year. If the bicycle rolls near the handle, you will watch it at home or with the family. On the opposite side of the cup indicates you may catch it on a business trip far from home.

Beginning on the left side of the handle, read the cup clockwise and look for patterns from past to future. Everything counts no matter how insignificant, and the placement of objects within a quarter inch of each other denotes a close relationship between events. Read the strongest patterns first, as the most distinct symbols reflect the greatest importance.

Letters usually represent the name of a friend or family member, and numbers mean time. Small dots indicate a journey, while larger clumps mean money well deserved. Wavy lines warn of uncertainty, and straight lines express a definite path. Circles spell success, and stars and triangles read as good fortune. Anything on the handle itself represents the diviner instead of the seeker, so if you see large clumps on the handle, don't forget to charge your client the enormous sum the leaves say you will get for your services.

The following list may help with content.

Angel - good news

Ants - many obstacles (or call Orkin)

Apple - achievement (unless you are Bill Gates, in which case it means danger)

Arrow - bad news in a letter (Does the image of a computer mean bad news in an e-mail?)

Ax - impending danger (or don't go into a dark basement when scary music is playing)

Ball - a desire to move

Basket - a pleasant surprise

Bell - news

Bird - good luck

Broom - out with the old, in with the new (or your house seriously needs cleaning)

Butterfly - happiness

Cage - marriage proposal (Honestly, that's what it says!)

Cat - a deceitful friend (obviously written by a dog person)

Compass - travel

Eyeglasses - look for a surprise (But then it won't be a surprise, will it?)

Faces - friendships

Gun - avoid quarrels (especially with people with guns)

Key - new interests

Ladder - advancement

Saw - obstacle

Snake - enemy (The Snake Slander Society, better known as SSS, is currently lobbying to repeal this interpretation. They claim they have been vilified unjustly throughout history because of an unwise fruit recommendation. Look for the complete transcript at www.throwahissy.org.)

Spider - secrets

Star - destiny

Straight line - journey

Tree - good health

Wavy line - frustration

Wheel - advancement

Windmill - grand schemes (or a trip to Holland in the future)

During a heat wave at the 1904 World's Fair in St. Louis, Richard Blechynden found no buyers for his tea. So, he put ice cubes in it and invented iced tea.

Today, the United States drinks more iced tea than hot.

Addison

The Garden Tearoom

15201 Midway Road
(Inside Unlimited Ltd. Antiques)
972-239-0395
http://www.unlimited-ltd.com

You know you are in a town with money when within a two-mile radius lies six golf courses, a private airfield, and three malls filled with such names as Saks, Nieman Marcus, Lord and Taylor, and Macys. Why not coast your Lear jet into Dallas and spend the day shopping with the beautiful people?

Direct your chauffeur to the north end of Midway where Antiques Unlimited has catered to the *nouveau riche*, with a yen for the old, for over thirteen years. If highboys make you happy and cherry china cabinets make you chipper, this place will put a smile on your face faster than you can say blue chips, with prices even your chauffeur can afford.

In between the sideboard sale and your bassinet binge, take a breather at the Garden Tearoom. Overlooking the showroom with the mahogany dental cabinet, the French provincial dining set, and the Roaring Twenties walnut suite, the padded maroon walls and stained glass windows add a touch of subdued elegance to the maroon table linens and green wrought iron chairs. Sip your Peach tea and save room for the specialty pies and cakes made from scratch daily. When nature calls, the "powder room" stands right next to the "necessary room." Apparently, men don't use powder and the women's room is not quite as necessary.

If you are due in Paris for cocktails, ship the furniture home and get your lunch goodies to go. Chocolate cream pie tastes twice as good at 30,000 feet.

House Tea: Peach

Hours: (Store) Mon.-Sun. 10-6; (Lunch) Tues.-Fri. 11-3, Sat.-Sun. 11:30-4:30

Location: Midway Road and Beltline

Extended Services: Wedding and Baby Showers, Rehearsal Dinners, Receptions

Menu

Salads

Garden Salad - Lettuce, tomato, and carrot with a house dressing

Chef Salad - Served with ham, turkey, boiled egg, cheddar and Swiss cheese

Sandwiches

Tuna Salad - With pecans, apples, and water chestnuts

Chicken Salad - With apples, raisins, celery, and walnuts

Turkey - On sourdough with sprouts and cranberry mayonnaise

Ham and Cheese - On rye with lettuce and tomato

Gourmet Grilled Cheese - With Swiss, American, and cheddar, bacon, and tomato

Pimento Cheese   Egg Salad

Archer City

The Cottage Tea and Antique Shop

105 N. Ash

940-574-4016

Close to Oklahoma, about where the wind comes sweeping round the plain, lies the town of Archer City and the little yellow house of the Cottage Tea and Antique Shop. Restored nine years ago by Harold and Bertie Beekman to showcase their antique furniture and cut glass collection, the turn-of-the-century box home now hosts a thriving tearoom. The pair runs the restaurant like a tag team; she cooks and he does the rest. Although Bertie changes the menu to fit her mood every day, the marinated chicken breast and famous chocolate meringue pie that put the tearoom on the map can be devoured daily among the white linens and candy-striped carpeting.

To digest your food, you can wander to the downtown strip where writer and prodigal son Larry McMurtry has converted four of the storefronts into his used bookstore, Booked Up. After years in the big city, Larry finally returned to the town on which he unflatteringly based *The Last Picture Show*. On any given day you can navigate your way through the shelves and find him stocking the recent acquisition of first editions. If you feel brave enough, grab a copy of *Lonesome Dove* for him to autograph. He's actually pretty down home about it, but that's the kind of town Archer City is.

> "Indeed, Madame, your ladyship is very sparing of your tea;
> I protest the last I took was no more than water bewitched."
>
> – Jonathan Swift

House Tea: Lemonade

Hours: Tues.-Fri. 11:30-2 (Reservations Only)

Location: West Pecan and Ash

Extended Services: Wedding and Bridal Showers, Rehearsal Dinners

Arlington

 ## The Rose Garden Tearoom

3708 W. Pioneer Pkwy (Highway 303)
(Inside Antiques and Moore)
817-795-3093

What would a garden picnic be without the sounds of birds singing in the nearby trees? At the Rose Garden Tearoom, bird song flutters in the air from grapevine branches with white twinkling lights. Birdbaths, trellises, and French café tables give this restaurant the air of dining on the patio in air-conditioned comfort.

Patrons are served garlic toasties and Rose Petal iced tea, the house specialty, in long-stemmed green glass goblets with a jaunty orange slice. Once you are seated, service is efficient and friendly, but the popularity of the spot can produce a long wait, especially on the weekends. If you don't have time for reservations, drop your name off and make one lap around both parts of the antique room floor. If you pause to pick a sweater for your teddy bear at the bear corner, ogle the estate jewelry, and stop to ponder why anyone would want a couch made out of camel pelvises, you will be back at the tearoom in just the right time to be seated.

39

Incidentally, the birds that you hear singing are finches from Sussex, England. They can sing in your house for just $9.95 if you buy the CD.

House Tea: Rose Petal (mix of rose petals, vanilla, and strawberry)

Hours: (Store) Mon.-Sat. 10-6, Sun. 12-6; (Lunch) Mon.-Sat. 11:30-4, Sun. 12-4

Location: Corner of Pioneer Parkway (Highway 303) and Park Springs

Extended Services: Wedding and Baby Showers, Rehearsal Dinners, Afternoon Tea

Menu

Salads

The Garden Salad - Gourmet lettuces, vegetables, and toasted pine nuts with house dressing

The "Loa Salad" - Tossed greens with pecans, fruit, grilled chicken, and special dressing

Sandwiches

Tuna Salad - On wheat bread with lettuce and mayonnaise

Sliced Turkey - On croissant with honey mustard or dill sauce

Chicken Salad - On brioche bread

Our Garden Club - On toasted wheat with turkey, cheese, bacon, ham, and lettuce

Vegetarian - Served with avocado (in season), cream cheese, sprouts, tomato, black olives, red onion, and special dressing on pita bread

Entrees

Garden Munchkins - Potato skins filled with spicy ground beef and cheddar cheese, served with sour cream and picante sauce

▓ The Garden Tearoom

1715 E. Lamar
(Inside The Antique Sampler Mall)
817-861-2760

Many people born in Fort Worth have never set foot over the Dallas city limit, and if you ask someone from Dallas to drive to Fort Worth, they'll look at you with an expression of horror that a stroll into the Everglades might evoke. Hunkered down between the two cities like a freshman at a fraternity food fight, Arlington enjoys the best of both worlds. Known primarily for the Six Flags theme park and the baseball stadium, imaginatively named "The Ballpark," Arlington shares its sister cities' activities while offering its own excellent parks, stage theaters, and choice agoras to whittle the paycheck.

One example of a singular shopping experience is the Antique Sampler Mall. Sister to the antique mall in Grand Prairie, this 55,000-square-foot building fairly bursts with vintage furniture, antique dolls, quilts, and sports memorabilia. Gerry, pronounced "Gary," Scholes owned the mall as well as the one in the old Coca Cola building, the first antique store in the area. After she sold it to her neighbor, Gerry was enticed from retirement to run the Garden Tearoom that resides just inside the mall.

Across from the Victorian christening gowns and parasols, puffy white clouds float in a watercolor sky over fountains, recessed windows, and ivy-covered walls. Originally, the tearoom's purpose was to give the shoppers a place to peacefully contemplate their $50,000 bedroom suite purchase. But, attracted by the monthly theme luncheons, the occasional live music, and a menu created by Chef Jim Sevenson, the Garden Tearoom now lures customers to the antique mall. And yes, they do sell their wonderful Apricot Cherry tea to take home. Enjoy.

House Tea: Apricot Cherry

Hours: (Store) Mon.-Sat. 10-7, Sun. 12-6; (Lunch) Mon.-Fri. 11-3, Sat. 11-4

Location: Off I-30, behind Hurricane Harbor

Extended Services: Wedding and Baby Showers, Rehearsal Dinners, Catering, Children's Dress-Up, Afternoon Tea

Menu

Salads

Smoked Turkey and Pasta - Smoked breast of turkey, seasonal vegetables, black olives, and rotini pasta

Almond Chicken Salad - Boneless chicken mixed with toasted almonds, sliced grapes, crisp celery, pineapple, and Tea Garden special dressing

Classic Caesar Salad - Caesar salad with homemade croutons and Parmesan cheese

Sandwiches

Traditional Club Sandwich - Triple-decker combination

Ham and Swiss Melt - Shaved ham, Swiss cheese, tomato, and sourdough bread

Chicken Salad Sandwich - White, tender chicken blended with grapes, celery, pineapple, seasoning, and special dressing

Veggie Wrap - Shredded greens, cheddar cheese, and seasonal vegetables rolled in a soft flour tortilla with a black bean pate

Entrees

Chicken Crêpes Supreme - Roasted chicken and mushrooms rolled into a crêpe and smothered with supreme sauce

Chicken Alfredo - Boneless breast of chicken tossed with alfredo sauce, linguini, and Parmesan cheese

Gulf Shrimp and Pasta - Shrimp tossed with linguini pasta, topped with diced tomato, special sauce, and seasonings

Wonderful World of Cooking

2400 West Pioneer Parkway
817-792-2002

When you hear the name "Wonderful World of Cooking," don't you just imagine sort of a Williams-Sonoma kitchen store; pots and pans hanging from the ceiling, a wall of bizarre kitchen implements, and a couple of bistro tables in the back? Well, you'll have to get your lemon zester someplace else because no cactus-shaped cookie cutters clutter the contemporary pastel walls of this tearoom. Instead, a bay window overlooks an alcove room with ferns in brass stands and permits the sunshine to brighten the seafoam green and dusty rose tables of the main room. Serene and unfrilly, Wonderful World attracts a varied clientele with its decor and robust entrees, including seafood crêpes and lasagna.

The owner, a former fourth grade teacher, admits that some of the friendly, white-smocked waitresses took her math tests years back and evidently lived to tell the tale. After a demitasse of hot gazpacho soup to cleanse the palate, they merrily appear with your salad plates so fast you'll wonder if they spotted you in the parking lot and pegged you for a tuna crunch-looking person.

If a Hilly Dilly onion cream cheese fit strikes you in the evening, Wonderful World provides an extensive list of special order catering and take-me-home-now delicacies, including water chestnuts wrapped in bacon, fruit kabobs, and chocolate-dipped strawberries. They will even prepare the food in your own serving dishes so you can pretend that you made it. And they won't tell a soul.

House Tea: Almond

Hours: (Lunch) Mon.-Sat. 11-2:30; (Order Pick Up) Mon.-Sat. 10-4

Location: Corner of Highway 303 and Bowen Road

Extended Services: Wedding and Baby Showers, Rehearsal Dinners, Catering, Afternoon Tea

Menu

Salads

Chicken Chutney Salad	Spinach Salad

Sandwiches

Reuben	Egg Salad
Crab-Mushroom Melt	Pimiento
Tuna Crunch with Melted Cheese	Walnut-Apple Chicken
Sliced Turkey, Ham, and Cheese on Croissant	

Entrees

Chicken-Broccoli Crêpe - With a béchamel wine sauce

Seafood Crêpe - Shrimp, crab, and a touch of broccoli

Sour Cream Chicken Enchilada - Tortilla filled with chicken in a creamy cheese sauce with a cheese and sour cream topping

Lasagna - Stuffed with Italian sausage, ground beef, and three cheeses

Chinese Chicken - With steamed vegetables over rice

Benbrook

 ## Palm Garden

9250 Highway 377 South
(Inside Benbrook Antique Mall)
817-249-5455

"If you don't get on that plane, you'll regret it. Maybe not today or tomorrow, but someday and for the rest of your life." The owners of the Palm Garden may not have intended their tearoom to resemble a watering hole in Casablanca, but they succeeded admirably. Sitting among the palms and Bedouin draping, you almost expect Peter Lorre to run in and hiss, "Rick, Rick, you have to save me."

At the back of the Benbrook Antique Mall, the puffy white clouds float on their painted tiles over the giant water ollas, rich peach swags, and the ornate latticework that encloses the room. Heavy mirrors and stained-glass windows adorn the walls. Every table bears a single exotic flower, and tiny Tiffany lamps cast a romantic glow over the two-tops. Potted palms discretely hide your assignation from onlookers. Palm Garden would be dramatically appealing on its own, but connected to the

Benbrook Antique Mall, it'll provide a perfect excuse to start antique collecting.

If you have some bucks to throw around, you can start your collection with the fifteen-foot coal fired, Atlantic 4-4-2 Steam Engine at the front of the store. Can't you just see yourself riding around the backyard on that during neighborhood cookouts?

House Tea: Cinnamon Orange

Hours: (Store) Mon.-Sat. 10-6, Sun. 12-6; (Lunch) Tues.-Sat. 11-3

Location: ¾ mile off Loop 820

Extended Services: Wedding and Baby Showers, Rehearsal Dinners

Menu

Salads

Palm Garden Salad - Mixed greens, assorted vegetables, and choice of dressing

Waldorf Chicken Salad - Served on a bed of mixed greens

Raspberry Garden Salad - Greens with seasonal fruits and roasted pecans with a raspberry vinaigrette and grilled chicken breast

Chef Salad - Greens and assorted vegetables, ham, turkey, cheddar cheese, and boiled eggs

Mediterranean Salad - Greens, Greek olives, feta cheese, red onion, tomato, green pepper, cucumber, and Greek dressing

Sandwiches

Chicken Salad	California Bacon, Lettuce, and Tomato
Tuna Salad	Smoked Turkey
Roast Beef	Ham
Roger's Reuben	Palm Garden Club

Entrees

Quiche of the Day	Loaded Baked Potato

Bowie

Shirley's Rose Garden Tearoom

116 East Pecan Street
940-872-6844

What could be more romantic than getting away for the weekend to a secluded bed and breakfast? A specially prepared dinner is served by candlelight; no kids, no chatter, no people hollering into a cellular phone at the table next to you, just you and your main squeeze. After dinner and a fine dessert, take a stroll along the country road past the old oaks. The surrounding town of Bowie is very quiet and peaceful. The bright city lights are gone, and the stars seem much closer. The air smells clean and fresh with a faint whiff of something sweet but unidentifiable, maybe jasmine or honeysuckle. After the walk, adjourn to your upper room hideaway, where the dim light, high ceilings, and luxurious comfort deduct a hundred years from your daily cares. The four-poster bed reclines across the spacious room and the dormers extend over the house, with windows overlooking the yard. A private reading area is tucked away in one corner, and the bathroom has an enormous antique claw-foot tub. Get lots of sleep. Tomorrow is a big day of antique shopping followed by Afternoon Tea when you get hungry.

> "Drinking at least 8 ounces of tea a day, whether hot or cold, appears to cut the risk of heart attack by 44 percent."
>
> – The Atlanta Journal, July 1999

The hideaway room is only one of the choices in this 1895 house turned bed and breakfast. The Jenny Linde Room downstairs, named for the type of furniture, is elegant, and the aptly named Queen Victorian Rose Room has a canopied bed so opulent you'll order servants to run your bath.

When Bill and Shirley Roberts first bought the house, most of it was already restored, but the 400-square-foot attic was just ducts and insulation. Bill built the hideaway as well as the stairwell. When it was finished, the couple asked Dorothy Powell of Dallas to decorate it with the same loving detail she did with the tearoom. The result is a refined, comfortable retreat for the body and soul.

Originally, the Rose Garden Tearoom only served Afternoon Tea. Recently they have extended their menu to lunch as well. Plans for a gazebo in the expansive backyard are already underway. Maybe when it's complete, you can do the *Sound of Music* dance routine in it with the partner of your choice and pretend you're sixteen going on seventeen.

House Tea: Rose Petal or Apricot

Hours: Tues.-Fri. 11-2

Location: Corner of Lindsay Street

Extended Services: Wedding and Baby Showers, Rehearsal Dinners, Children's Dress-Up, Afternoon Tea, Bed and Breakfast, Special Dinner and Stay Packages

Burkburnett

 Victoria's Garden Tearoom

119 E. Third
(Inside Burkburnett Antique Mall)
940-569-5363

On the way from Wichita Falls to Oklahoma City is the town of Burkburnett, affectionately called "Burk" by the natives. Downtown in what was once the Boyd's Dry Goods Store and connecting bank building is now the Burkburnett Antique Mall and Victoria's Garden Tearoom. This 1908 building was built during the town's boom and now houses the antique mall that specializes in Victorian collectibles.

As you look up the ivy-covered railing that leads to the tearoom from the antique mall, Jane Hill, the owner of Victoria's, welcomes you from the balcony. Upstairs, the intimate room is the main dining area, but for guests who have a difficulty with steps, several tables are thoughtfully provided in the quiet alcove at the foot of the staircase.

The landing of the stairs features miniature porcelain dolls partaking of their own tea. The water fountain and the ivy in the main dining area give the room a garden party air, and the mauve table linens and covered chairs add an elegant touch.

Jane Hill, a former teacher, began directing Victoria's while working full time. Eventually she stopped teaching to run the tearoom. Even she admits that the restaurant is more work. Jane says that when she is finished running the restaurant, she'll write a cookbook for all of those people who keep asking her for the secret recipe for her trifle.

House Tea: Apple and Ginger Peach

Hours: (Store) Tues.-Sat. 10-5:30, Sun. 1-5; (Lunch) Tues.-Sat. 11-2

Location: Downtown

Extended Services: Wedding and Baby Showers, Rehearsal Dinners, Receptions, Catering

Menu

Salads

Chef Salad   Dinner Salad

Sandwiches

Roast Beef Sandwich   Seafood Salad Sandwich
Chicken Salad Sandwich   Tuna Salad Sandwich
Ham and Cheese Sandwich   Chicken Salad on Croissant
Seafood Salad on Croissant   Ham and Cheese on Croissant

Burleson

 ## The Peppermint Tearoom

101 W. Ellison Street
817-447-2323

When the owners of what one day would be the Peppermint Tearoom first looked at their acquisition, they wondered what they had gotten themselves into. The 14,000-square-foot historic site in downtown Burleson was previously a bar, infamous for the teenage cruising crowd. Years of neglect made the restoration of this lovely old building a challenge. Friends helpfully suggested they bulldoze the place and start from scratch. Neighbors were just grateful that the headbanger music had stopped. The new owners set to work, and two years later the Peppermint Tearoom became the favorite spot of local groups and folks just looking for a little peace and quiet. In their honor, no background music is played in the tearoom. The upstairs, originally slated to be an art gallery, now holds receptions and formal affairs. The downstairs has an enclosed tearoom and a separate alcove area that is perfect for meetings.

New Yorker, Thomas Sullivan, stitched his tea into silk sachets and thus invented tea bags.

Originally square, tea bags later became round, then pyramid-shaped, then back to square

The most coveted item on the menu, chicken and dumplings, was once a special of the day that the owner added to lure men to the tearoom. Originally, it was only served on Saturday, but it was in such demand that the folks at the local Seventh Day Adventist Church asked the tearoom to please feature an additional day so that they, too, could partake. Now, chicken and dumplings are devoured Tuesday, Thursday, and Saturday. If you want some, you'd better get there early. That dish is more popular than Toll House cookies at a college dorm.

House Tea: Orange

Hours: (Store) Mon.-Sat. 10-6: (Lunch) Mon.-Sat. 11-3

Location: Bailey's One Main Place

Extended Services: Wedding and Baby Showers, Rehearsal Dinners

Kreative Tea Parties

109 W. Ellison Street
(Inside Nashville, Texas)
817-295-9580

In the back of the Nashville, Texas antique store in downtown Burleson, you can "join the Queen for tea." Owner Lorena Bowles has spent years doing children's dress-up tea parties in style. Once an owner of her own tearoom, Lorena closed her shop when her children were born and started the freelance children's tea party service she runs today. Recently Lorena moved the location of her parties from the Peppermint Tearoom next door to this new location.

For authenticity, Lorena's parties cannot be surpassed. Miniature tables and chairs, china, napkins, and silver candelabras make the adults feel like they just got off the train in Lilliput but are just perfect for children. For Her Majesty's Tea, girls have authentic Lillie Ruben and Oscar de la Renta gowns with matching gloves, hats, and the costume jewelry of their choice. Boys have top hats, officer hats, and bushy mustaches to don. Her Majesty, of course, wears a rhinestone tiara and a crushed velvet robe with white satin trimming and sits in a royal chair presiding over her court.

The cuisine includes Chocolate Soup (chocolate ice cream and chocolate syrup) and sandwiches made with Over the Rainbow bread, a locally baked bread in all the colors of the rainbow. The children can participate in a fashion debut, photo session, etiquette lessons, and a horse-drawn carriage ride through Burleson, where the art of waving in a queenly fashion is sure to be mastered.

And just when you are thinking you wish you were a kid again, never fear, adults can participate too. At the mother/daughter teas, kiddo gets to pick mom's hat, and at the Daddy's Little Princess Teas, dad chooses from an assortment of fuzzy lipwear. If you don't have a child but always wanted to wear a tiara for your birthday party, Kreative will be sure to accommodate you.

House Tea: Lemonade

Hours: (Store) Mon.-Sat. 10-6, Sun. 12-5; (Lunch by reservation) Mon.-Fri. 10:30-5:00, Sat. 10:30-5:45, Sun. 12:15-5:00

Location: Bailey's One Main Place

Extended Services: Children's Dress-Up

Canton

 The Tearoom on the Square

131 S. Buffalo
903-567-6221

Say the words "first Monday" and every antique enthusiast within a
ten-mile radius will shout "Canton" in decibels of adoration. Canton's First
Monday Trade Days is legendary throughout the antiquing community.
Held during the weekend of the first Monday of each month, the miles of
Trade Day booths would require at least the entire weekend just to scan
the offerings. Real shopping requires a concentrated game plan and a great
pair of sneakers. Trade Day veterans are easily spotted with their deter-
mined expressions, collapsible carts filled with purchases, and water
bottles slung over one hip. They came early in the morning to get the best
deals and beat the afternoon heat. They grab the morning parking spaces
so they can reload the trunk throughout the day with treasures. They
weave through the antique furniture, quilting supplies, vintage games,
yard ornaments, china, and railroad paraphernalia like pros, searching for
that Woody Woodpecker glass or rare Tarot deck to complete their
collection.

Every month the supply changes at the trade ground as merchants bring their overstock and seconds to the free-for-all, and the permanent vendors show off their new finds. Whether you are looking for a matching knob for your Louis XV étagère or a tapestry pillow with Pomeranians, Canton is *the* place to find it.

With all the to-do about Trade Days, don't overlook the town of Canton itself. Scattered with antique and bric-a-brac stores, this little town offers a big dose of hospitality to the droves of out-of-towners who descend upon it monthly. One such find calls itself the Tearoom on the Square. This quiet, elegant oasis allows you to quench your parched throat with a goblet of Almond tea that tastes like a liquid version of Chinese restaurant cookies.

Inside the high walls of this 1893 mercantile, maroon and white walls extend to the arched doorway of the kitchen. Strategically placed counters and glass cabinets tantalize guests with views of the chocolate meringue pie and other goodies. Very naughty of them! Opposite the entrance, flanked by potted spiral junipers, a mahogany sideboard with a mantel clock covers the wall. Tables are dressed in refined white and sport vintage teapots or unusual vases from The Very Thing antique store two doors down. The Saxtons run this store as well as the tearoom, so they can rotate the decor whenever they feel so inclined. But they intentionally keep the look clean and uncluttered to rest the eyes from the visual overload that usually accompanies trips to Canton.

A plethora of sandwiches and specialty soups are offered daily, but for a change of pace try the spinach salad made with strawberries and toasted almonds with a strawberry poppy seed dressing.

If you don't already have plans, try to get to Canton during their Fourth of July celebration. The old-fashioned parade with antique cars, scout troops, and decorated bicycles will put you in the proper nostalgic mindset for the rest of the festivities. The precision lawn mower brigade is a must-see. Proud homeowners propel their patriotically wrapped Snappers and Toros to the beat of a John Philips Sousa march. Not to be outclassed, the lawn chair drill team is a riot. Perhaps high school bands should add this feature to their half time spectaculars.

House Tea: Almond

Hours: Mon.-Fri. 11-2, (Sat. 11-2 on first Monday weekends only)

Location: On the Square

Extended Services: Wedding and Baby Showers, Rehearsal Dinners, Receptions, Weddings, Afternoon Tea

Menu

Salads

Chicken Salad	Tuna Salad
House Salad	Spinach Salad
Tuna Salad in a Tomato	Chicken Salad in a Tomato
Grilled Chicken Salad	Hawaiian Grilled Chicken Salad

Sandwiches

The Grilled Alamo - Thinly sliced turkey, avocado, tomato, and provolone served on Parmesan bread

Hearty Club on Croissant - Roast beef, Swiss, turkey, lettuce, and tomato

Grilled Chicken on Croissant - With melted Swiss cheese, lettuce, and tomato

Tearoom Melt on Croissant - Turkey, bacon, ham, and cheese

Turkey Deluxe on Sourdough - Thinly sliced turkey with bacon, Swiss, lettuce, tomato, and grilled purple onion

Turkey Avocado Melt on Croissant - Thinly sliced turkey, avocado, sprouts, Swiss cheese, lettuce, and tomato

Tearoom Croissant - Filled with roast beef and topped with melted provolone cheese

Roast Beef	Tuna Melt
BLT Sandwich	Ham Sandwich
Turkey Sandwich	Chicken Salad
Tuna Salad	Veggie on Wheat
Club Sandwich	Grilled Cheese

Entrees

Quiche of the Day	Baked Potato Royale

The longer the infusing, the more the caffeine. The smaller the leaves, the faster the caffeine extracts into the water.

Corsicana

 Off the Beaton Path

211 S. Beaton
903-874-5767

Where else besides Beaton Street could you expect to find the Beaton Path Antiques and its next-door neighbor, Off the Beaton Path Tearoom? Behind the floor-to-ceiling stained glass window, liberated from an English church, the former oil rush hotel offers a refined afternoon lunch to the people of Corsicana. Grapevines woven with flowers and fairy lights twinkle over maroon and green tables with ice cream parlor chairs. Here and there designer teapots, many of them donated by customers, perch on shelves.

Off the Beaton Path's reputation for chicken salad precedes it, but the chicken spinach quiche and blackbottom cheesecake should not be ignored. Iced Raspberry Zinger typically remains the house favorite, but for the sentimental, the Mom Pettiette Twist iced tea, named after the owner's grandmother, features an old-fashioned sugar and lemon flavor that will make you homesick even if you aren't Southern. If in a hurry, you can order your tea in the frozen to-go package. Beaton's makes their ice

55

cubes from the tea itself, so you can pop a few in a cup, drive around for ten minutes, and presto, iced tea.

If you get the chance, visit the Collin Street Bakery. The guided tour through the factory will provide you with enough fruitcake facts to astound your friends and neighbors at Christmas and possibly win a game show.

House Tea: Raspberry Zinger

Hours: (Store) Tues.-Sat. 10-5; (Lunch) Tues.-Sat. 11-2

Location: Seventh and Beaton

Extended Services: Wedding and Baby Showers, Rehearsal Dinners

Menu

Salads

Chicken Tropical - Sliced chicken breast on a bed of lettuce, topped with pineapple, Mandarin oranges, almonds, and honey mustard

Top Hat Chicken Salad - Chicken salad served on a bed of lettuce

Sandwiches

Off the Beaton Path - Avocado, tomato, mushrooms, provolone cheese, and lettuce on a croissant

Main Street Attraction - Cathy's secret sauce served on a croissant with sliced turkey, cranberry, and lettuce

Nick's Favorite - Turkey on wheat bread with cheese, tomato, and lettuce

Marvelously Mad Chicken Salad - Served on a croissant

Entrees

Crêpe à la Mornay Raspberry Vinaigrette Salad - Chicken and mushrooms rolled in a crêpe and covered with Mornay sauce

The finest tea is SFTGFOP, which stands for Special Finest Tippy Golden Flowery Orange Pekoe.

Dallas

 The Adolphus Hotel

1321 Commerce Street
(Inside the Adolphus Hotel lobby)
214-742-8200

If memories were ghosts, you could stroll through the opulent Louis XV lobby of the Hotel Adolphus and greet the specters of celebrities who once graced this downtown Dallas jewel. Created by beer baron Adolphus Busch at a time when cattle was king and the new wealth from cotton and oil lured movie stars to this young, thriving city on the Trinity, the twenty-one-story Adolphus towered over the city, dazzling onlookers with bronze statues, intricate mansard roofing, and elaborately carved facades. It even had air conditioning.

Step past the doorman and through the brass doors, and you've entered another era where the shimmering souls of the bygone past seem right at home among the mahogany paneled walls. As you saunter over the plush floral carpet past the gilt frames of ancient kings and palms in Oriental pots, you can imagine Tallulah Bankhead descending the intricately carved golden stairs, her long opalescent gown rippling over the forest green carpet. Among the palms at the bottom of the stairs stands Rudolph Valentino in his sheik's garb awaiting her arrival.

As you move into the chandeliered lobby that once boasted the Century Room, big band music echoes from decades past. The carpeted floors once clicked to the rhythm of couples swinging to Tommy and Jimmy Dorsey's bands. Glenn Miller played here as well as Harry James, Dizzie Gillespie, and the Andrew Sisters. Visiting celebrities of the thirties and forties were invited to come on stage and join the band for a set, much to the crowd's delight. When the song ended, the crowd returned to their tables as the floor retracted under the bandstand. Olympic winner Dorothy Franey glided into the spotlight on the hidden sheet of ice as she did for fourteen years.

Cross the lobby and peek in the glittering French Room, where the swell of murmuring voices and clinking glasses bounces off the vaulted muraled ceilings. Cherubs flit among the clouds over the seventeenth-century crystal chandeliers, heavy draperies, and rococo moldings in glittering gold. Wall sconces cast a glow over the starched white table linens and fine porcelain china, illuminating the faces of chatting diners as they did when Roosevelt and Douglas MacArthur, Carter, Haig, and LBJ all sipped their port and discussed foreign policy across the round tables. You don't have time to join them; the Queen expects you for Afternoon Tea.

In the vast lobby, Liberace plays some of his favorites on the magnificent Guggenheim Steinway. Bing Crosby croons softly as you sink into a deeply cushioned chair under one of the colossal tapestries while Prince Philip helps himself to a watercress sandwich and some strawberries. The Queen accepts the Villeroy and Boch teacup from Sir Ian McKellan and nods her agreement to Eleanor Roosevelt, who just remarked that women are like tea bags. The tea today is Harvey and Sons Earl Grey, just like at home-sweet-castle, and the Queen is pleased. And when the Queen is pleased, everyone is pleased. Help yourself to a scone with raspberry marmalade and a chocolate truffle or two. Van Cliburn will start playing in a few minutes. Life doesn't get much better than this.

House Tea: Harvey & Sons

Hours: (Tea) Wed.-Sat. 3-5

Location: Downtown

Extended Services: Afternoon Tea, Hotel

Café Avíon

6500 Cedar Springs Road
(Inside Love Field Antique Mall)
214-351-9989

Crank the Corvair and start the Studebaker, the Antique Car Club is on the roll to Café Avíon for their weekly filler-up. Nestled between the Love Field Antique Mall and the Classic Car Museum, Avíon is patronized by antique shoppers, car buffs, and airline pilots who can phone ahead from the plane as they land across the street.

Of course the café carries an aviation theme. Pictures of vintage aircraft dot the walls. Tables are dressed with an international city theme; baguettes, jars of olive oil, and of utmost importance, Toblerone hazelnut chocolate bars sit at center stage. Perrier bud vases adorn the checkered tablecloths, and Pelgrinos stand by for the thirsty tourist.

Avíon serves heartier food as well as tearoom dainties to cater to the diverse crowd it draws. French wine stew and artichoke chicken with rice frequently appear as daily specials. The bread pudding gets rave reviews, but it you really want a memorable dessert, go next door and buy one of the classic Corvettes.

House Tea: Raspberry

Hours: (Store) Mon.-Sat. 10-7, Sun. 11-6; (Lunch) Mon.-Sat. 11-3

Location: At Mockingbird and Cedar Springs

Extended Services: Wedding and Baby Showers, Catering, Afternoon Tea

Menu

Salads

Homestyle Tuna Salad - Combination of spring water-packed tuna and spices

Waldorf Salad - Chunks of chicken with herbs, spices, apples, raisins, and walnuts

South Grilled Chicken Salad - Romaine lettuce and Parmesan cheese mixed with dressing and grilled chicken

Classic Grilled Chicken Caesar - Crisp Romaine lettuce, Parmesan cheese, Caesar dressing, and croutons

Chardonnay Salad - Romaine, tomato, onion, and Mandarin oranges blended with a Chardonnay and caper dressing

Sandwiches

Curried Turkey and Ham - Turkey, ham, and cheese flavored with a curry cream sauce

Mexican Melt - Melted Mexican cheese with tomato, avocado, and lettuce

Café Club - Ham, turkey, bacon, Swiss cheese, lettuce, and tomato

Grilled Chicken Club - Grilled chicken breast, lettuce, tomato, bacon, and cheese

Chef's Tortilla Roll - Tortilla with ham, turkey, Swiss cheese, lettuce, and tomato

Pimento and Cheese   Homestyle Tuna
Chicken Waldorf   BLT Classic

Entrees

Quiche of the Day - Custard, onion, cheese, and spices in a flaky crust

Salmon Cakes - Salmon, green pepper, and herbs

Chicken Artichoke - Chicken breast and artichokes in a creamy sauce served over rice

French Country Beef Stew - Beef, carrot, and onion, with a brown country wine sauce over noodles

Hot Roast Beef - Roast beef with mashed potatoes and vegetables

Meatloaf - Served with mashed potatoes, gravy, and vegetables

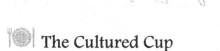

The Cultured Cup

5346 Belt Line Road
972-960-1521
http://www.theculturedcup.com

When it's cold and rainy in Texas (both days), it is always pleasant to crank the Mozart and curl up in an overstuffed chair with a cup of your favorite blend and a tin of shortbread. A visit to the Cultured Cup will provide you with everything you need for these times, except the Mozart and the chair.

Between the narrow walls of this eighteen-year-old business, the Cultured Cup treats visitors to a wide variety of coffee and some of the best teas the world has to offer. On one long wall, a virtual smorgasbord of teas line the shelves in neat little tins. The Cultured Cup features over thirty varieties of Mariage Frères and Fauchon of France for the connoisseurs in all of us. If you don't know which type appeals to you, perch on the bistro barstools at the back of the store and allow them to serve you a sample in an antique porcelain cup, or attend one of their periodic tasting classes. On the register lies a schedule of their upcoming

Tea Talks, such as the "Royal Shenanigans and High Jinks Through the Ages" tea talk. For these occasions, the counters are pushed back and the affair is catered in white linen style. If you feel especially adventurous, visit a tasting seminar of European Drinking Chocolates. You haven't lived until you've tried this ultra-decadent cup of cocoa heaven.

Along the shelves of the long, windowed wall are massed a collection of designer teapots, chocolate pots, decorated sugar cubes, shortbread, strainers, and anything else needed to prepare you for that cold, rainy day. Remember, shortbread calories consumed while drinking tea don't count—they are offset by the caffeine.

House Tea: Thirty varieties

Hours: (Store) Mon.-Sat. 10-6

Location: Beltline Road between Montfort Drive and Preston Road, in the Addison Town Hall Square

Extended Services: Tea Classes, Tastings, Catered Tea Talks

 **Jennivine**

3605 McKinney
214-528-6010
http://www.dallasdinesout.com

At the busy intersection of McKinney and Lemmon Avenue is Jennivine, "a little bit of England in Dallas." Jennivine was created twenty-three years ago by the Indian-born daughter of a British architect, hired to design the Grand Palace of the Maharaja of Jodhpur. Jennifer Lejeune left her job as one of London's top fashion models to search Dallas for the perfect location to plant her excellent restaurant. She chose a turn-of-the-century house that was once a bar and a blue jeans shop. Named "Jennivine" for the extensive international wine list, including Silver Oak Cabernet Savignon 1995, Charles Shaw Chardonnay, and Chalk Hill Cabernet Savignon 1993, this renowned restaurant is usually frequented for its gourmet brunch, lunch, and dinner, which converts Texans from barbecue to Brie.

Following the custom of both India and England, Jennivine also serves a fabulous, formal Afternoon Tea. They provide the outrageous hats, the multiple courses of finger sandwiches, petit fours, and a tea punch that will knock your socks off. The

Afternoon Tea was supposedly started in the 1840s by Anna, the 7th Duchess of Bedford, who needed a Snickers break before the standard 8 P.M. dinner hour.

punch is a combination of berry tea, La Creme, fruit, cinnamon, and boiled rum. The folks at Jennivine would tell you the other secret ingredients, but then they'd have to kill you. But hey, what's life without a little mystery!

Inside the house, the dark woodwork and maroon accents transport you to Victorian England. Outside, the Union Jack flying next to the front door and the bright red "tele" booth suggest that you are in England, but the potted jalapeño plants on the tables are a dead giveaway.

If the weather is nice, the covered porch with its white lights and lovely flowers is heavenly. If you haven't the time to perch for a while, call in advance for the Mad Hatter Light Lunch Carry Out. It is like a formal tea on wheels. You provide the linen tablecloth for your car.

House Tea: Rotates daily

Hours: (Lunch) Tues.-Sat. 11:30-2:30, 6-10 P.M.; (Tea) Tues.-Sat. 2:30-5

Location: McKinney and Lemmon Avenue

Extended Services: Wedding and Baby Showers, Rehearsal Dinners, Afternoon Tea, Afternoon Tea to Go

Lady Primrose

500 Crescent Court
214-871-8334

"Who is this Lady Primrose and why is she sending postcards to you?" one
jealous woman asked her husband. He couldn't answer, because he didn't
know. When Carolyn Hunt and Vivian Young decided to open their English
antique store, they sent 2,200 postcards of thatched cottages in England to
everyone they could think of. Each card said:

> Having a wonderful time *Shopping English Countryside*. See
> you in October.
>
> Love,
> Lady Primrose

The marketing idea was to promote their new store, Shopping English
Countryside, which featured lovely antiques and gifts. The store was
designed to feel like a little bit of Britain come to Dallas. But the name
didn't stick, and when the tearoom was moved to the first floor, the owners
renamed it to Lady Primrose. Now, Lady Primrose is one of the few places
that specializes in formal Afternoon Tea and has won the Best Tea Service
award by *Tea Quarterly Magazine*.

Inside, the restaurant is an eyeful of flounces, flowers, ivy, and thatched cottage roofs. Chimes made from silver tea services suspend from the ceilings. Diners in secluded alcoves recline in comfortable floral upholstered chairs. The petit fours and finger sandwiches are served on lazy Susans with delicate doilies. The hot tea is served in antique pots with silver strainers by waitresses with properly starched pinafores. The whole mood is so refined you will come out with an English accent.

Despite that, Lady Primrose is definitely not stuffy. Centrally located, it has become the hub for local businesswomen doing power lunches and political powwows. In the words of Vivian's favorite writer, Oliver Wendell Holmes, "much has been shared over the teacups."

House Tea: Secret Garden (mix of peaches, cinnamon, and hibiscus)

Hours: (Lunch) Mon.-Sat. 11:30-2, (Tea) Mon.-Sat. 3-5, (Brunch) Sat. 9-11

Location: Inside the Crescent Court at 2200 Cedar Springs and Maple

Extended Services: Wedding and Baby Showers, Rehearsal Dinners, Receptions, Afternoon Tea, Afternoon Tea to Go

Menu

Salads

Fresh Field Greens - Served with Stilton cheese

Prawns and Spinach Salad - Served with orange avocado dill vinaigrette

Caroline's Chicken Salad

Sandwiches

Bombay Curried Chicken Sandwich - Served with Waldorf salad

Entrees

Ham Wensleydale - Served with apple potato salad and green beans

Westminster Chicken Crêpes - Served with lemon herb sauce and Kew Garden salad

Secret Garden Platter - Served with angel hair pasta

Thatched Cottage Tart - Served with field greens salad

Mary Ellen's Old-Fashioned Tearoom

138 Spring Creek Village
972-386-9080

As you approach the corner of Spring Creek Village, you can hear lively chatter fill the air. Laughter, the sound of clinking silverware, and provocative aromas rise from the shady breezeway. Scattered around brick planters of topiaries and petunias, wrought iron bistro tables are filled to capacity with corporate professionals grabbing a few moments for lunch. Waitresses bustle to and fro, serving icy glasses of their Peach tea to the crowds on the patio and those basking in air-conditioned comfort.

Inside, the daylight streams through the front windows and onto the sunflowers adorning the tables. The sunflower motif is repeated in the table linens, planter boxes, and around the walls throughout the rooms. The front room is intimate, but there are several larger areas toward the back for busy afternoons and the group functions that are frequently here.

Before lunch, guests are treated with a demitasse of hot gazpacho soup and some cheesy fish crackers to cleanse the palate. For a main course, Mary Ellen's is known for its tuna and chicken chutney salad, but the heavier board of fish Creole, chicken divan, and meat ravioli assures the patronage of menfolk. If you go for lunch during the week, be sure to get there early. Mary Ellen's bustles with corporate professionals from the nearby silicon corridor.

House Tea: Apricot

Hours: Mon.-Sat. 11-2:30

Location: NW corner of Coit and Beltline

Extended Services: Wedding and Baby Showers, Rehearsal Dinners, Catering, Takeout

Menu

Salads

Exotic Crunchy Chicken Chutney Salad - Served with choice of fruit, garden, or spinach salad

Zippy Tuna - White tuna served with fruit, garden, or spinach salad

Weight Watcher's Delight - Zippy tuna made with light mayonnaise and a pineapple slice with cottage cheese

Scrumptious Spinach Salad - Spinach topped with turkey, cheese, bacon, mushrooms, and house dressing

Sandwiches

Turkey Croissant - With homemade dill or honey mustard dressing

Mary Ellen's French Dip - Roast beef with mozzarella cheese and onion

Sliced Roast Beef on a Sesame Bun - Served with lettuce, tomato, and American cheese

Hot Tuna Melt on a Croissant - Served with melted mozzarella cheese

Chicken Walnut Apple   Tuna Crunch
Homemade Pimento Cheese   Egg Salad

Entrees

Chicken Divan - Breast of chicken slightly curried over broccoli and topped with toasted bread crumbs

Meat Ravioli - Made with ground sirloin and ground Italian sausage and topped with meat sauce

Lasagna - Made with Italian sausage, ground sirloin, cheese, and meat sauce

Fish Creole - A filet of orange roughy baked in a Creole sauce made with a variety of Cajun spices and green peppers

Quiche of the Day - Served with fruit, garden, or spinach salad

S&S Tearoom

260 Inwood Village
214-351-6888
http://www.sscatering.com

The oldest surviving tearoom in Dallas was also one of the original businesses in Highland Park Village. S&S Tearoom, named after the two sisters who created it, opened its doors in 1931 just down the street from the Highland Park Theater. Handed down only two times in its seventy-year history, this tearoom still maintains a large portion of its original recipes even though the service has expanded to include three square meals and a catering business.

In its current location, S&S nestles among the art galleries and eclectic shops of the Inwood Village Shopping Center. The patio with its wrought iron tables and great view of the surrounding stores gives guests the perfect chance to people-watch. Inside, the maroon velvet chairs, still-life paintings with gilt frames, and heavy gold drapes lend an aristocratic air to the tableau. It is easy to see why this tearoom has been the darling of the white-gloved bridge crowd since the 1930s. Although S&S has grown well past the four-table business with which it started, this family-owned restaurant has maintained its original ambiance. Perhaps this is why new generations continue to discover its charms already known to veterans—good food, good company, and killer cinnamon rolls. S&S

proudly observes a traditional Afternoon Tea with fresh breads, scones, and petit fives (one level better than petit fours).

House Tea: Strawberry Apricot

Hours: Mon.-Sat. 7 A.M.-9 P.M., Sun. 8-2:30

Location: At the back of Inwood Village Shopping Center

Extended Services: Wedding and Baby Showers, Rehearsal Dinners, Receptions, Catering, Afternoon Tea

Wonderful World Café

6023 Sherry Lane
214-750-0382

A tearoom filled with men? What's wrong with this picture? Absolutely nothing if you are at the Wonderful World Café. The quiet Czech-owned restaurant is a favorite meeting spot for doctors and businessmen from nearby hospitals. Although it has a thriving delivery business, many prefer a leisurely lunch in the comfortable, unfrilly dining room. Decorated conservatively with high-back chairs and simple, elegant linens, this tearoom has a homey Old World feel.

The eclectic spread appeals to a wide variety of tastes. Along with the standard tearoom choice of salads and quiche, the menu boasts pimento

69

cheese sandwiches, green chicken enchiladas, chicken chutney, and an interesting sandwich made of turkey, apples, and Havarti cheese. The specials are French country cookery, and each lunch is served with an herbal tomato broth apéritif.

Wonderful World draws a wide assortment of clubs. The table layout is a natural for business meetings and showers, and several sororities hold their functions here. If you stop by on Wednesday, say hello to the "Roosters." This group of cutthroat domino players has been meeting here for years.

House Tea: Apricot

Hours: (Lunch) Mon.-Fri. 10-5, Sat. 10-3, (Tea) Mon.-Sat. 1-4

Location: At Preston Center

Extended Services: Wedding and Baby Showers, Rehearsal Dinners, Receptions, Catering, Afternoon Tea, Delivery

Menu

Salads

Chicken Salad Almondine - Chicken salad accompanied by congealed salad (that's Jell-O with a graham cracker crust) and cheese puff sandwich

Southwestern Cobb Salad - Romaine lettuce, chicken, avocado, jicama, tomato, bacon, Cotija cheese, and toasted pumpkin seeds with homemade bread

Chicken Artichoke Caesar - Crisp romaine with chicken breast, croutons, and artichoke hearts with Caesar dressing and a cheese puff sandwich

Sandwiches

Croissant Sandwich - Turkey or ham with Swiss

Preston Center Sandwich - Smoked turkey, dilled Havarti, chutney mayonnaise, and apple slices on marble bread

Entrees

Chicken Wine Mushroom - Baked breast of chicken in a light mushroom sauce with rice pilaf and vegetables

Country Pot Roast - Hearty lunch with vegetables and mashed potatoes

Meatloaf - A traditional blend of beef and vegetables with homemade gravy, mashed potatoes, and a vegetable

Green Chicken Enchiladas - A California dish with chicken, spinach, and green chilies in a mushroom sauce

Roasted Vegetable Plate - Roasted seasonal vegetables and rice pilaf

Chicken Spaghetti - Combination of chicken, tomato, celery, onion, and peppers

Vegetable Lasagna - Low-fat version of the classic favorite

Southern Savory Chicken Casserole

 The Zodiac Room

1618 Main Street
(Inside Neiman Marcus)
214-741-6911
http://www.neimanmarcus.com

In 1907 when Herbert Marcus, Carrie Marcus Neiman, and Al Neiman first opened their apparel store in downtown Dallas, they didn't expect it to become the Shangri-la for the fashion elite as it is regarded today. They wanted a store of women's ready-to-wear in a time when most of the clothes were created by personal dressmakers. The oil fields started booming, and their customers demanded luxuries that only recently they could afford. One woman came in barefoot with a worn calico dress and asked for a mink coat. She bought the coat and paid with a crispy $10,000 bill. Her family's farm had just struck oil.

It was Stanley's marketing ideas that created the Neiman's legend we know today. He established fashion shows during the 1920s to educate the market. Models floated through the store aisles wearing the latest designer creations. Celebrities were invited to visit the store and given an Award for Distinguished Service in the Field of Fashion. Soon, Neiman's name became associated with elegantly attired actresses like Grace Kelly.

The Zodiac Room upstairs was built after an expansion in the fifties for out-of-town customers to dine while shopping. The restaurant, with its twenty-foot pueblo watercolor, quickly took on a life of its own, becoming famous for its culinary masterpieces and heritage cuisine.

The Zodiac offers Afternoon Tea at its locations in Dallas and Houston. You can nibble on a scone and hobnob with the near great and near, near great and check out what the anorexics are wearing in Paris this year. The sales clerks only ask that you not drool on the Judith Leiber purse counter. It's so unladylike.

"Twinkle, twinkle little bat!
How I wonder what you're at!
Up above the world you fly,
Like a tea tray in the sky."

– Lewis Carroll

House Tea: Black Current

Hours: (Lunch) Mon.-Sat. 11-3; (Tea) Mon.-Sat. 2-4

Location: Corner of Commerce and Ervay Street, downtown

Extended Services: Wedding and Baby Showers, Rehearsal Dinners, Catering, Afternoon Tea

Denton

 ## The Chestnut Tree

107 W. Hickory Street
940-591-9475

Across from the court-house in downtown Denton, you can "go through the Garden Gate to the Chestnut Tree." As you walk over the threshold of this unusual combination of garden store and tearoom, a myriad of bright flowers and agri-gifts surround you. Vine-laden trellises cover the walls, and buckets of dried flowers line the walkway. A selection of desktop water fountains, garden paraphernalia, and other gifts for the horticultural enthusiast fill the room.

Steer past the foliage and step around the distressed farm windows that lead into the Chestnut Tree tearoom. Eclectic tables, some painted in vivid Mary Engelbreit-type designs, gather around the wooden floors. The ceiling fans churn overhead, and a fountain gurgles in the corner.

The Chestnut Tree is known for its creative entrees and desserts and has published its five-year anniversary cookbook with recipes ranging from brandy cheese balls to Bavarian pot roast. The recipes are from innovative specials that change weekly. The very best selections are recorded in this cookbook for you to try at home.

House Tea: Raspberry

Hours: (Store) Mon.-Sat. 10-5:30; (Lunch) Tues.-Sat. 11-2:30

Location: Across from the courthouse in downtown

Extended Services: Wedding and Baby Showers, Rehearsal Dinners, Receptions, Catering

Menu

Salads

Garden Greens	Caesar
Fresh Fruit Plate	Chicken Salad
Tuna Salad	Club (Ham, Turkey, Cheese)
Grilled Chicken Caesar	Chef's Favorite

Sandwiches

Chicken Salad - Chicken breast with almonds and special seasoning

Tuna Salad - Served with onion, celery, and mayonnaise

Egg Salad - Served with onion, celery, and mayonnaise

Turkey and Cheese - Mesquite smoked turkey with Swiss cheese

Club - Mesquite smoked turkey, ham, and Swiss cheese

Roast Beef - Served on a grilled bun

Veggie Pita - Tomato, zucchini, yellow squash, mushrooms, carrots, and cheese on a whole wheat pita

Veggie Wrap - Avocado, cucumber, tomato, provolone, sprouts, and mayonnaise

Duncanville

 Cretia's Flour and Flowers

215 West Camp Wisdom Road
972-298-9888

Close your eyes anywhere on Camp Wisdom Road and let your nose lead you to Cretia's Flour and Flowers. From blocks away, tantalizing smells of vanilla, rum, and cinnamon propel your feet into this bakery turned tea-room. Beware, Cretia's is not for strict dieters. Just the smell alone will make you gain ten pounds.

As you walk in the front door, perch yourself on a barstool and let them make you the coffee drink of your choice. (Yes, they say the "c" word here.) Lined along the back of the bar are huge glass jars of every kind of coffee bean you can imagine, as well as biscotti and other unidentified pastries of Italian descent.

When you are ready for a "real" drink, the tearoom is around the corner past the bakery. Although it is tempting, don't get hypnotized by the Bavarian tortes, key lime tarts, and Black Forest cake. Just tell yourself that good things come to those who wait, and pull up a chair in the tearoom. A cup and saucer already awaits you on the table. Pick one most appealing. They are all different and all antiques.

The handful of elegant tables gather intimately on the other side of the coffee bar room divider. Diners can enjoy the sunshine pouring through the storefront windows while they sip their Strawberry Kiwi iced tea and devour the homemade scones. The scones are made exclusively for the tearoom and not sold at the bakery. If you think it is a crime to eat the butter meticulously carved into a rose, try the clotted cream instead. Just make sure you leave room for dessert. And remember, you can always jog home.

House Tea: Strawberry Kiwi

Hours: Mon.-Fri. 11-2, Sat. 11-3

Location: Corner of W. Camp Wisdom and Duncanville Road

Extended Services: Wedding and Baby Showers, Rehearsal Dinners, Catering, Wedding Cakes, Bakery, Coffee Bar

Ennis

 ## English Tearoom

101 S. Dallas
972-875-3995

Ennis has long been a best-kept secret to Texan antiquers and railroad enthusiasts. But this historical town, filled with restored turn-of-the-century buildings, is also home to several excellent festivals, including the Train Festival and the National Czech Polka Fest in May. Whether you are there for the shopping, the motor speedway, or to jump on the Bluebonnet Trail, be sure to save some time for lunch in downtown Ennis.

Across the street from the burnt remains of what used to be the Ennis Emporium is the new Downtown Emporium. Once a CR Anthony department store, this revitalized building is now home to multiple gift shops, clothing boutiques, and most especially, the English Tearoom.

When you walk in the front door and into the airy, spacious atrium, you can see why Pat Jenkins decided to close up shop at the Main Street Tearoom and move to this lovely new location. Lining the balcony are the beveled glass French doors of the boutique shops that offer Brighton, Michael Simon, and That's Me fashions to name a few. The tearoom sits in the center of the downstairs foyer where the light from the front windows gives it a cheerful French bistro feel. The tables, chairs, and other furnishings are classical English mahogany, and the linens and seasonal decorations are upscale.

The English Tearoom is known for its excellent peach crêpes, but even if you don't have time to stop for a bite while shopping through downtown Ennis, just standing in the atrium and inhaling the aroma of freshly baked croissants is enough to make your entire day.

House Tea: Peach and Raspberry

Hours: Tues.-Sat. 10-4, Dinner by reservation on Thursdays

Location: On the main street through town

Extended Services: Wedding and Baby Showers, Rehearsal Dinners, Receptions, Catering

Menu

Salads

Side Salad   Citrus Chicken Salad
Garden Salad

Sandwiches

Adorned Chicken Salad   Traditional Tuna Salad
Ham and Swiss   Turkey Cranberry

Wildflower Café

211 W. Knox
972-878-6868

Peppered among the antique stores in downtown Ennis sits Interior Ideas and the Wildflower Café, an unusual combination of tearoom and interior design store. The brainchild of the mother and son team of Betty Glaspy and James Robinson, the two stores cohabit in perfect harmony. For twenty years Betty Glaspy has run Interior Ideas, offering tasteful choices in fabrics, wallpaper, and furniture to folks seeking helpful advice for their home decorating. When her son expressed his desire to run the Wild-flower, the partnership was struck and the café has been a success ever since.

The Wildflower, called "café" not "tearoom" so men won't balk at the doors, is decorated with the same *objets' d'art* as the rest of the store that surrounds it. The recessed alcoves and throw pillows nicely compliment the wood floors and dark green Victorian wallpaper. The effect is very homey.

A portion of the Wildflower's clientele comes from the nearby Euphoria Day Spa. A popular haunt for tourists who wish to pamper themselves, Wildflower provides the much-needed sustenance after the body wraps and Swedish massages.

Before you leave, don't forget to check out the studio of Juan Schlegal in the back of the store. The bluebonnets and back roads paintings of this area artist are tremendously popular and have been featured in several books spotlighting the nearby Bluebonnet Trail of Texas.

House Tea: Peach

Hours: Mon.-Sat. 11-2

Location: Downtown

Extended Services: Wedding and Baby Showers, Rehearsal Dinners, Catering, Takeout

Menu

Salads

Chef Salad - Served with ham, turkey, and cheese

Spinach Salad - Served with hot bacon dressing

Adorned Chicken Salad - Served with mixed fruit and walnuts

Sandwiches

Chicken Salad   Classic Club
Ham and Swiss   Turkey on Toast
California Club

Yellow Rose Bed and Breakfast and Tearoom

204 W. Belknap
972-878-0682

Whether in Ennis for the Kolache Christmas or the races, the Yellow Rose Bed and Breakfast and Tearoom finds rest and sustenance for weary travelers. For years, Joel Hardell and his wife visited B&Bs throughout the country, and when they retired the couple decided to build a place for their friends to visit. The pair found a house one block from downtown and converted it to a sunny yellow house with white trim.

Each of the rooms carries a flower theme as befits the name of the house. The relaxing Blue Willow Room and the cheerful Yellow Sunflower Room are arranged with antique furniture collected by the couple for many years. The proprietress's love for all things Victorian prompted the creation of the tearoom. Primarily used for children's dress-up tea parties, the room also serves as the dining hall for their guests and the local bridge club's game location of choice.

The lady of the house is a huge tea fan, but Joel admits that although he's been out of Wisconsin for twenty-five years, he's just now beginning to like tea. He is, however, very fond of cheese.

House Tea: Wild Strawberry

Hours: By reservation only

Location: Two blocks from downtown

Extended Services: Wedding and Baby Showers, Rehearsal Dinners, Receptions, Children's Dress-Up, Weddings

Farmersville

 ## Sugar Hill Tearoom

101 McKinney Street
972-784-6121
http://www.farmersvilletx.com

In the 130-year-old Rike Drug Store in Farmersville resides the Sugar Hill Tearoom, designated for the town's original name before an infamous bar-room brawl forced a separation of the surviving parties. The two-story Victorian with the original facade and windows serves as a gift shop, tea-room, and the home of the owners. The gift shop fills the downstairs with candles, picture frames, miniature tea sets, and firehouse collectibles, one of the owner's favorite themes. Next to it, the tearoom in dark rose, cherry woods, and forest green fattens locals with its signature dish, caramel banana cream pie. Daily hot specials, like Southwest chicken casserole, pepper the menu. (Only in a small town could you get turkey with jalapeño jelly sandwiches or ham with peach jam on a croissant.)

While you're planning your calendar, pencil in the first Saturday of October when Farmersville presents Old Time Saturday. This day of barbecues, bands, and gunfights celebrates the town's origin with a bang.

House Tea: Cherry Vanilla

Hours: Tues.-Fri. 11-3

Location: On the Square

Extended Services: Wedding and Baby Showers, Rehearsal Dinners, Catering

Menu

Salads

Fruit   Pasta
Spinach   Garden

Sandwiches

Chicken Salad   BLT
Ham/Swiss with Peach Jam   Turkey with Jalapeño Jelly
Club   Veggie

Entrees

Quiche of the Day   Baked Potato

Forney

Back in the Olden Days

10694 West Highway 80
(Inside Memories, etc. Antiques Mall)
972-564-2188

A few years back, Governor Clements declared Forney the "Antique Capital of Texas." Whether this was due to Clements Antiques, owned by his brother in said town, was never mentioned. This rural community does boast a large percentage of dealers, however, including the Memories, etc. Antiques Mall on Highway 80.

One day while Rhonda DeVilbiss shopped at Memories, she spied an empty space with a kitchen in the back. Out of self-admitted nosiness, she asked the mall owner what they intended to do with the open space. The lady told her she was looking for a new owner for a tearoom they wished to create there. Rhonda said, "Pick me, pick me." The rest is history as they say.

Enclosed by armoires, sideboards, and English dressers lies the cozy Back in the Olden Days Tearoom. Two-tops, some decoupaged by the owner, scatter around the floor surrounded by basic wooden chairs. Despite the visitors along Highway 80 traveling to and from Shreveport, Arkansas, and Oklahoma, most of the Olden Days repeat business comes from locals who like things simple. So Rhonda maintains the clutter at a minimum, the bread white, and the tea straight up. Even so, she manages to sneak gourmet recipes under unpretentious names.

> "No! Ne'er was mingled such a draught in palace, hall or arbor, As freemen brewed and tyrants quaffed that night in Boston Harbor."
>
> – Oliver Wendell Holmes

Her fabulous cherry soup, made with diced cherries, sour cream, and cherry wine is actually a borsht in disguise as is the peach and papaya mango soups she serves in summer. Since she actually had a customer return the gazpacho because it was cold, she also serves creamy tomato, made the old-fashioned tedious, but delicious, way and a basic lemon chicken soup. The earthy bread, which serves as the specialty of the house, comes from a little bakery in Plano that whips up the white, wheat, spinach parmesan, and cranberry orange creations daily. Her apple pie comes with or without brandy sauce in deference to the religious convictions of her customers. But the raspberry brownie with pistachio ice cream should be listed as a cardinal sin. The next time you pass through Forney, drop by and try that cherry borsht. Just don't call it that in front of the other customers.

House Tea: Orange Pekoe

Hours: (Store) Mon.-Tues., Thurs.-Sat. 10-5, Sun. 12-5; (Lunch) Mon., Thurs., Fri. 11-3, Sat.-Sun. 11-4

Location: On the access road at the Talte exit

Extended Services: Wedding and Baby Showers, Rehearsal Dinners, Catering

Fort Worth

 Secret Garden

2601 Montgomery Street
(Inside Montgomery Antique Mall)
817-763-9787

The bleary-eyed man peered out the door at the visitors. The estate sale wasn't until 7 A.M., but at 6 A.M. he had two couples on his porch glaring at each other competitively. When the garage door went up, all four people moved in for the kill, outbidding each other to prevent the others from buying the furniture. At the end of the day, that bleary-eyed man was a much wealthier man. Several estate sales later, both couples admitted that the competition was becoming expensive. They decided to collaborate and later became friends.

When the Ben Hogan Golf Factory vacated the warehouse across from the engineering firm where one of the gentlemen worked, the couples decided to buy the building. They opened "Texas's Largest Antique Mall,"

83

complete with a tearoom that would not only encourage the visitors to stay during lunch, but would attract a crowd based solely on its own merit.

Today, in a quiet clearing tucked away from the clash of customers wildly searching for missing pieces of their discontinued china patterns, sits the aptly named Secret Garden. Graceful and quiet, the tearoom allows weary shoppers to sip their Apricot Mango tea and compare their purchases. The area is spacious enough for showers and receptions and even for one wedding, which was held there for a couple who met in the tearoom. The dim lighting and the friendly staff instantly bring the blood pressure down and provide a lovely haven to enjoy a bite of lunch or a bit of biscuit and creme.

House Tea: Apricot Mango

Hours: (Store) Mon.-Sat. 10-6, Sun. 12-6; (Lunch) Mon.-Sat. 11-4, Sun. 12-4; (Tea) Mon.-Sun. 2-4

Location: I-30 at Montgomery

Extended Services: Wedding and Baby Showers, Rehearsal Dinners, Afternoon Tea

Menu

Salads

Queen Victoria's Greek Salad - Spinach with mushrooms, onion, and feta cheese with a traditional Greek dressing

Palace Penne with Pesto and Vegetables - Chilled pasta tossed with spring vegetables and basil dressing

Foreign Intrigue Thai Salad and Peanut Sauce - Sweet and spicy dressing over lightly seasoned vegetables, chilled angel hair pasta, and a blend of herbs topped with chicken

Lady Emma's Fruit Salad - Served with lemon poppy seed bread

The Queen Mother's Chicken Waldorf - Chicken salad with grapes, apples, and pecans

Sandwiches

The Queen Mother's Chicken Waldorf - Chicken salad with grapes, apples, and pecans on whole wheat

The King's Courtyard Tuna Salad - Tuna salad with celery, boiled eggs, and special spices on whole wheat

Prince Harrison's Roast Beef and Swiss - A French roll with Dijon horseradish sauce and Swiss cheese

Lady Elizabeth's Smoked Turkey and Swiss - On whole wheat bread with basil mayonnaise

The Crown's Favorite Vegetarian - On croissant with avocado, sprouts, carrots, cucumbers, bell peppers, and tomato with a dill cream cheese and provolone cheese

Entrees

Sir Christopher's Quiche Florentine - A light blend of eggs, cheeses, mushrooms, spinach, and cream

The Secret Garden Quiche - The chef's mood-inspired composition

Saint Matthew's Lasagna - Three cheeses, Italian sausage, spinach, and a tomato sauce

Gainesville

 ## California Street Tearoom

111 W. California Street
940-665-6540

Just a hop, skip, and a jump from the outlet mall is an interesting foray into history and a really terrific tearoom. Once known as Magnolia's and then as Carrie's, this historic JC Penney mercantile building now plays home to the California Street Tearoom and Miss Pittypat's Antiques. The ground floor of the spacious building that houses the antiques once was the actual department store. Customers would select their purchases and then, in order to complete the transaction, the clerk would have to run up the wooden stairs to the loft that overlooks the showroom floor. The cash registers perched at the top of the stairs, as did the clerk's boss, keeping a watchful eye over his employees and the customers. When the order was rung up, a clerk attached it to the metal chain that ran between the order loft and a tiny, isolated loft on the other side of the floor. There, the accountants sat and calculated all day without contact with customers or other employees. Makes you appreciate your job, doesn't it?

Today the order loft is the California Street Tearoom run by the tag team of Shamaria Edington and Teresa Clark, the Cagney and Lacey of the tea world. Best friends for many years, the two decided to take over the tearoom and update its services. On one side of the room under ivy-covered ceilings sit antique cabinets, where a fine selection of coffee and loose tea can be purchased. The furniture includes Amish farm tables, flour mill cabinets, and antique furniture inherited from the old JC Penney mercantile. Several pieces are curiosities. The display cabinet that now acts as a counter obviously began life as some sort of department store storage crib, but its original purpose still remains a mystery. If you are an antique authority, stop by and enlighten the owners of its past use. They would really like to know.

House Tea: Almond

Hours: (Store) Mon.-Fri.10-5:30, Sat. 10-6, Sun. 1-5; (Lunch) Mon.-Sat. 11-3

Location: On the square

Extended Services: Wedding and Baby Showers, Rehearsal Dinners, Receptions

Menu

Salads

Pesto Pasta Salad	House Salad
Caesar Salad	Amaretto Chicken Salad

Sandwiches

Chicken Salad Sandwich	Garden Veggie
Cream Cheese and Turkey	

All of the thousands of tea varieties are named after the region in which they grown, the fermentation process, or what is blended with them.

Garland

 Potpourri Cottage

113 N. 6th Street
972-272-2625

Outside Dallas the family-oriented city of Garland puts on a good show any time of year. The four-day Fourth of July celebration features a different music group in the park each night, fireworks, crafts, a midway full of rides, and most importantly, a set of misters to spray the throngs who attend this midsummer bash. In October, Garland sponsors a fiddler's contest and chili cookoff. The merchants dress in pioneer clothing, and exhibitions of butter churning, rope making, and spinning flax fill the park. The first weekend in December, Santa Claus gives the reindeer the day off and takes his Santa-copter into downtown. There, he patiently records the wishes of acquisition hopefuls while surreptitiously updating his naughty/nice list. You can't buy much with coal these days, so make sure you're on the "A" list.

In whatever season you visit Garland, take time to visit the Potpourri Cottage across from the Opera House downtown. A cornucopia of gifts and collectibles fills the front of the 100-year-old five and dime. Check out the "Texas" smelling candle tins with scents including country clothesline, boots and saddles, cowboy coffee, and mesquite campfire. One customer remarked that her husband was a fireman, and when he's out of town, she burns the campfire candle because that's how his clothes smell when he gets home at night. She burns the coffee candle because she says it reminds her of his breath. Now that's love!

The tearoom in the back exudes tranquillity with every bird chirp. The white latticed Magnolia room sports porch lamps on the brick cutaway wall. Ivy, old-fashioned hats, and twinkling lights lend this alcove the air of a southern plantation patio. The main room with the puffy cloud ceiling and garden mural changes with each occasion. For bridal luncheons, the tables reflect the wedding colors while white tulle and flowers bedeck the bride's chair. Rattles adorn the centerpieces for the baby showers, and graduates celebrate in the colors of the school they recently escaped from. The garden mural on the side wall was painted by co-owner Marcia Lewis, who calls herself the "silent partner" because she lives in Lubbock. Her sister, Kaye Fitzhugh, runs the Cottage and calmly extends her hospitality to the multitude of lunch guests and private functions that keep the pinafored waitresses bustling.

The most popular item on the menu is the Cottage Croissant with turkey, cranberry sauce, and orange dressing. But don't miss the white cheddar and asparagus soup when it rotates on the daily specials list. For those who believe that the word "tearoom" is actually a euphemism for "dessert," save room for the coconut cream pie or the chocolate chip pecan pie served with whipped cream and chocolate syrup drizzle. For those on a diet, the key lime pie and blackberry or peach cobbler should do the trick. True, these desserts have just as many calories, but they contain fruit and that has to count for something.

House Tea: Raspberry, Orange Spice, Cranapple, Guava Peach, or Ginger Peach in rotation

Hours: (Store) Mon.-Sat. 10-5:30; (Lunch) Mon.-Sat. 11-2:30

Location: Downtown

Extended Services: Wedding and Baby Showers, Rehearsal Dinners, Receptions

Menu

Salads

Spinach Salad - Spinach, Mandarin oranges, toasted almonds, and poppy seed dressing

Pasta Salad - A combination of pasta, seasonings, and creamy honey mustard dressing

Tuna Salad - Albacore tuna with apples, walnuts, celery, onion, and dill pickles

The Hen's Nest - Chicken, celery, fruit, and pecans in a special dressing

Sandwiches

Chicken Salad	Tuna Salad
Ham and Monterey Jack	The Cottage Croissant

Graham

Magnolia Tearoom

523 Fourth Street
(Inside Serendipity Antiques)
940-549-8000

For all of you history junkies, Graham should be your next weekend adventure. Perched in the epicenter of the Forth Worth-Wichita Falls-Abilene triangle, the little city of Graham knows how to show visitors a big time. Where once dilapidated shells stood in place of the thriving downtown businesses, now exists the fully restored National Theatre. Originally built in the 1920s when movies were an event complete with orchestra, dancers, newsreels, and cartoons, the theater has recently regained its lavish Art Deco design. First-run films project on the main screen and on the two others, the Staircase Theater and the Northstar, carved out of the adjoining buildings. The seats are vintage-comfy, the light fixtures authentic, and the crying room, a glass enclosure next to the projector room, gives your little crumb-runner a space "where no one can hear them scream."

If the 1920s seem about thirty years out of date, you should love the drive-in movie theater still operating after all these years. Rent that station wagon, throw the kids and the sleeping bags in the back (not necessarily in that order), and watch concession foods march around the screen, led by a hot dog doing backflips. It's pure nostalgia overdose.

When you plan your day in Graham, don't forget to pencil in lunch at Magnolia Tearoom inside Serendipity Antiques. Magnolia dishes its King Ranch casserole from its roost in the 1800s hardware across the square from the National Theatre. Surrounded by glam-rusted fencing, the floral tables dusting the wooden floors sit about where the nail cribs would have been 150 years ago.

In addition to their regular menu, Magnolia offers an imaginative bill of fare. Chilled soups including avocado, cucumber, or cantaloupe temper the furnace of summer, while the chicken tortilla adds both kinds of heat to the winter. Whatever you do, make room for the Pumpkin Delight. This pie with batter and pecans sold out so often as a guest dessert that it became a staple. Why wait for Thanksgiving?

House Tea: Magnolia Blend

Hours: (Store) Tues.-Sat. 10:30-5:30; (Lunch) Tues.-Sat. 11-2 (desserts till 3)

Location: On the north side of the square

Extended Services: All Private Parties by request

Granbury

Merry Heart Tearoom

110 N. Houston Street
817-573-3800

No place in Texas fairly bursts at the seams with history like Granbury, the 1850s Indian outpost named in honor of the Confederate hero buried here. From the 1891 courthouse with its always accurate, original tower clock, to the railroad depot, jail, and opera house, Granbury is a window into a bygone age. This frontier hamlet is chock-full of restored buildings and houses from the 1800s, mostly clustered around what *Texas Highways* magazine voted the "Best Town Square in Texas." The cabin of Davy Crockett's widow and son was built here on land granted to them by the Republic of Texas for Davy's bravery at the Alamo. Granbury was also the deathbed site of the man who confessed to be John Wilkes Booth. He inadvertently recovered, however, and disappeared, leaving the alleged assassination gun in his boardinghouse room wrapped in news clippings of Lincoln's murder.

When it is time to take a breather, cross the square to the 1905 mercantile that now belongs to the Merry Heart for a spot of tea and some gourmet chow.

Named for the proverb, "A merry heart hath a continual feast," this lovely tearoom reflects the spiritual nature of its owner. The front room is filled with curiosities, some Christian in nature, some just absorbing. Calligraphy sets with real quills sit next to a phrenology bust. Vintage hats line the tops of cabinets, which are filled with Vidalia onion mustard and Scorned Woman cheese straws.

The tearoom, tucked in the back, seats two floors of delicate tables and high-backed booths with green-glass lawyer lamps. The booths are from the 1930s drugstore that occupied the corner of the square. Under the black and green floral tablecloths, they still bear the carvings of decades of malt-slurping teenagers. You might check to see if there are any names you recognize.

The Merry Heart offers lunches, three types of Afternoon Teas, specialty tea parties like the Mad Hatter Tea or the Texas Tea, and most recently, dinner. Whether you are in town for the Civil War Reenactment or the Cowboy Heritage Festival, stop by. But check your spurs and bayonets at the door.

House Tea: Plantation Mint

Hours: Mon., Tues., Thurs. 11-3; Fri.-Sat. 8 A.M.-9 P.M.; Sun. 8-6

Location: On the west side of the square

Extended Services: Wedding and Baby Showers, Rehearsal Dinners, Receptions, Afternoon Tea

Menu

Salads

Garden Salad - Gourmet lettuce with vegetables and toasted seasoned nuts

Grilled Chicken Chef Salad - Santa Fe style chef salad with special dressing

Pasta Salad - A medley of fuscilli pasta and creamy dressing

Tropical Chef's Salad - Warmed ham and pineapple, cheese, pecans, garden greens, and a special dressing

Sandwiches

Chicken Salad or Tuna Salad   Sliced Turkey on Toasted Croissant

Tuna and Avocado on Croissant Chicken and Avocado

Avocado Olé - Avocado, cheese, onion, tomato, sprouts, and special dressing

Entrees

King Ranch Chicken Crêpes - A flavor of the Southwest

Tearoom Favorite - Chicken breast with American cheese, sautéed mushrooms, and tomato

Omelet - Cheese or Spanish served with toasted croissant

"Green tea may be useful in
controlling inflammation from injury
or diseases such as arthritis."
    – Boston Globe, April 1999

Grand Prairie

 ## The Willow Room

2985 Highway 360 #160
(Inside the Antique Sampler Mall)
972-602-3602

Tearooms inside antique malls are practically an institution. But some gain a life of their own that transcends the surrounding business. The Willow Room is such a place. Filling the upstairs of the Antique Sampler Mall, the Willow Room has become a mainstay for clubs, showers, and most especially, weddings.

Although having a wedding in an antique store may seem a bit odd, many couples choose the location to tie the knot because they met there, or are members of the Antique Auto Club that frequents the tearoom, or just because the Willow Room with its entrance staircase looks so elegant when spruced up for the big event. With its broad, curved rails bedecked in flower sprays and ribbons, even wedding photographers have been known to drool. The bridesmaids and woman-in-white descend the winding staircase to the landing below, where the vows are exchanged. When it is time for the rings, the couple pulls the ribbons suspended from the balcony. The wedding bands tumble from the bows. After the I-do's and the two hours of photographs with the in-laws, the party ascends to the Willow Room for the reception.

Inside the tearoom, a full-size carousel horse gallops toward an archway draped with white twinkling lights. The visual space appears open, but encompassed by columns and ficus trees, diners can observe shoppers without the feeding-in-a-fishbowl impression. Several larger group tables are surrounded by two-tops tucked into niches that inspire private conversations. The mahogany tables and chairs, floral linens, and china are refined, and the atmosphere is convivial but peaceful.

Many clubs, including the Antique Auto Club, favor the Willow. From every direction collector cars rumble into the parking lot, filling it to capacity. The proud owners admire each other's handiwork and then adjourn to the tearoom to swap transmission war stories and devour the zucchini walnut and strawberry mini-muffins served by the basket to each table.

For a small fee, Willow will provide special cookie placecards made by a local cake decorator. This edible art of sugar cookie and fondant icing comes in every kind of design imaginable. Teapots, 3-D flower baskets, envelopes, even old cars can be used as place settings. The names of the diners are air-brushed in icing. They are so pretty, the guests often don't want to eat them. Be sure to buy an extra one for everyone to sample.

House Tea: Apricot Cherry

Hours: (Store) Mon.-Sat. 10-6, Sun. 11-7; (Lunch) Tues.-Fri. 11:30-3, Sat. 11:30-4, Sun. 12-4

Location: Highway 360 at Mayfield

Extended Services: Wedding and Baby Showers, Rehearsal Dinners, Receptions, Catering, Weddings

Menu

Salads

Smoked Turkey and Pasta Salad - Smoked breast of turkey, vegetables, and tri-colored rotini pasta on a bed of lettuce with choice of dressing

Almond Chicken Salad - Tender chunks of chicken mixed with toasted almonds, sliced grapes, celery, and honey mustard dressing

Chicken Caesar Salad - Caesar salad with Parmesan, homemade croutons, olives, and breast of chicken

Waldorf Chicken Salad - Tender chicken mixed with apricots, apples,
poppy seeds, celery, green onion, toasted almonds, and Dijon dressing

Sandwiches

Traditional Turkey Club Sandwich - Breast of turkey, bacon, Swiss and
cheddar cheeses

Almond Chicken Salad Sandwich - Chicken salad with lettuce and
tomato

Fresh Veggie Wrap - Shredded garden greens, cheddar cheese, seasonal
vegetables, and black bean pâté rolled in a soft flour tortilla with a mild
salsa and Dijon mustard

Entrees

Gourmet Baked Potatoes - Served with choice of butter, sour cream,
chives, cheddar cheese, broccoli florets, bacon, mushrooms, and salsa

Grapevine

 Let's Pretend Tea Cottage

326 S. Main
817-421-6678

For a memorable day with your child, take a trip to Grapevine, home of
shopping Shangri-la, the Tarantula train, and Let's Pretend tea parties.
The morning's exercise regime begins at the colossal Grapevine Mills
mall. Warm up with a sprint from your parking space in El Paso to the front
entrance, and you'll be all primed and ready for your laps around the outlet
mall. Huge numbers hang over the starting gates so you can count down
how long you have left to suffer. Your heart hasn't received this much
exercise since you were given three minutes to make a connection at
DFW airport. When you pull up in front of the Rain Forest Café, you will
definitely be ready for a relaxing ride on the rails.

   The depot of the beautifully restored steam locomotive the *Tarantula*,
sits on Main Street in downtown. You can watch the train turn around in
the 1927 Santa Fe railroad turntable before boarding, then puff down to the

Fort Worth Stockyards for your cattle fix. For lunch, chug back to Let's Pretend in Grapevine.

In the 100-year-old general store across from the park gazebo, this tearoom caters to adults and children alike. The regular menu offers combination plates of sandwiches, soups, including the house tomato basil, and the quiche of the day. Pretend specializes, however, in children's tea parties, which have their own choice of delicacies. The Birthday Tea provides petit fours with candles, tea sandwiches, fruit kabobs, and cookies. The birthday girl becomes the guardian of the teapot and can wear the "party princess tiara" for the grand waltz up Main Street. Mother-Daughter teas are scheduled every Saturday, and special holiday teas, like the Nutcracker Tea for Christmas and the Miss Spider's Tea in October, are lavishly executed. If you don't have a child of your own, I'm sure there are several parents who would gladly rent one out to you for the afternoon. Just check around.

House Tea: Paradise

Hours: (Store) Tues.-Sat. 10-5:30; (Lunch) Tues.-Fri. 11-2; (Tea) Tues.-Sat. 3-5

Location: Downtown

Extended Services: Wedding and Baby Showers, Children's Dress-Up, Mother-Daughter Teas

Simple Pleasures

214 E. College Street
817-488-3291

When you get to the house with the steaming teapot in the front yard, you have arrived at Simple Pleasures. Once the night office of a turn-of-the-century dentist, this lovely house was built by his wife's father as a wedding present. Now the McCasland mother and daughter team bring their considerable expertise to it as a tearoom.

At one time the pair owned the Grapevine Gift Shop, a card shop not far from their present location. They thought it would be a good idea to put in a couple of tables and serve tea. Apparently their customers agreed with them, because the service became very popular. Soon folks were asking for sandwiches. Sandwiches led to soup and then to an antique and tearoom business. When the house on College Street became available, the McCasland ladies opened Simple Pleasures.

As a desirable place for showers, club meetings, and even a wedding or two, Simple Pleasures allows their guests to choose themed rooms in which to enjoy their lunch, such as the Garden Room, the Blue Room, and Mary's Room, named after an antique dealer who used to work there.

Of particular fame is the buttermilk pie. Given as a recipe when her son was born, the pie was only made at special holidays but is now clearly one of the most coveted items on the menu. Although Lynda McCasland admits that she never tasted it during all those years she baked it, now the recipe is a closely held family secret, known only to herself and her daughter Sandy, who spends most of her time whipping up new recipes in the kitchen. Don't bother to try bribery, their lips are sealed.

House Tea: Peach, Raspberry, or Tropical in rotation

Hours: (Store) Mon.-Sat. 10-6; (Lunch) Mon.-Sat. 11-2; (Tea) Mon.-Sat. 3-4

Location: Right off Main Street in historic downtown

Extended Services: Wedding and Baby Showers, Rehearsal Dinners

Menu

Salads

Garden - Mixture of Romaine and leaf lettuce, shredded carrots, and red cabbage sprinkled with sunflower seeds

Spinach - Red onion, Mandarin oranges, bacon bits, and Parmesan cheese

Pasta - Rotini pasta, zucchini, squash, red onion, and bell pepper tossed with Italian dressing

Sandwiches

Sandy's Chicken Salad - Chicken, celery, almond, curry, and soy sauce

Lynda's "New" Tuna - Tuna, hard-boiled eggs, celery, green onion, pecans, and sweet relish

Rita Mae's Egg Salad - Hard-boiled eggs, green onion, green olives, and a touch of black pepper

Health-Nut - Cream cheese, finely chopped radishes, and Greek seasoning served on Health-Nut bread with slices of cucumber and tomato

Hot Ham and Cheese - Honey baked ham and Swiss cheese

Haltom City

◉ The Lone Star Tearoom

4105 Denton Highway
(Inside Lone Star Antique Mall)
817-485-9341
http://www.lonestarantiquemall.com

Deep in the heart of Texas lies the Lone Star Antique Mall and Tearoom. Actually, Haltom City is geographically somewhere around the clavicle of Texas, if the eyes are located near Amarillo, and Brady lies somewhere around the navel. Despite its name, you won't find any spurs or saddles at the tearoom except during the Stock Show, when Lone Star swaps its British gentility for cowboy chic, and even the harp wears a Stetson.

Across the spacious, lush dark green carpet, the fashionable furnishings of the Victorian yesteryear lie in intimate vignettes. In the corner, high-backed gold velvet chairs and a mahogany tea table offer an alternative to the floral tables. A floor harp draped in white roses and gauze complete the scene. Against one wall, a fireplace mantel strewn with lace and china serves as a backdrop to Windsor chairs. Seated guests enjoy the protection from nonexistent flames by a scrolled brass spark arrester. The glow from vintage light fixtures reflects off the cream and gold striped wallpaper tastefully arranged with designer prints in gold frames. Ceiling fans keep the conversation circulating.

Of special interest on the menu is the southern pecan chicken salad, which comes in a sandwich or stag. The soups and entrees rotate daily and for special theme lunches, like the Valentine's Day spread. When you swing by, don't forget to give your congrats to Jennifer and Ronnie Raesz, the couple who own the mall and tearoom. They just got hitched.

House Tea: Pineapple Banana, Raspberry Cream, Apricot Mango, and Peach Vanilla in rotation

Hours: (Store) Mon.-Thurs. 10-6, Fri.-Sat. 10-7, Sun. 12-6; (Lunch) Tues.-Fri. 11-2, Sat.-Sun. 12-3

Location: Denton Highway and Stanley Keller Road

Extended Services: Wedding and Baby Showers, Rehearsal Dinners, Receptions, Children's Dress-Up

Menu

Salads

Fresh Garden Salad	Southern Pecan Chicken
Tuna Salad	Fruit Salad

Sandwiches

California Wrap - Wheat tortilla with blend of meat, veggies, and cream cheese

Club Sandwich - Ham, turkey, bacon, cheddar cheese, Swiss, lettuce, and tomato

Southern Pecan Chicken Salad Sandwich - Chicken breast, pecans, pickle relish, and special seasonings

Ham and Cream Cheese	Tuna Sandwich

The oldest living tea shrub is 1,700
years old and is near Burma.

Kaufman

 Especially for You Tearoom

100 W. Grove Street
972-932-4274

Picture yourself walking the
streets of Kaufman in the
early 1900s. You lift the hem
of your heavy skirt to cross
the dirt road while scores of
rickety cars careen past you,
their horns bleating. A break
in traffic occurs, and your
laced boots stride across the
street, careful to avoid the
piles of horse manure. A gust
of wind catches the brim of
your oversized hat and pulls
against your hatpins.

You stride past the post
office and climb the marble
stairs of the First National
Bank. Through the towering
doorway and into the cool,
damp interior you pause at
the teller cages. Light shines
through the stained glass
windows and reflects off the perforated ceiling tiles. Outside, the sand
gusts against the tin roof with metallic pings. The man with a white shirt
and black armbands gathers keys and escorts you to the heavy black vault
at the back of the room. He spins the dial and turns the big wheel. As the
door swings open, the words "Halls Safe and Lock Company, Cincinnati
and St. Louis" catch your eye.

The bygone days of the oil gushers are long past, but the First National
Bank still stands tall on the corner of the square. Now it houses the Especially for You Tearoom. The marble walls, tin roof, and stained glass
windows are all original. Even the vault remains intact, but now it holds a
deposit of bath supplies. A collection of gifts occupies the front room

where the tellers transacted business, and framed photographs of Kaufman's early days dot the walls.

The tables of the tearoom nestle in the winding catacombs at the back where the offices used to be. Antique lace from the owner's grandmother covers each private table. The oiled original floorboards squeak nostalgically as you move among the tables. The party rooms in the adjoining building are best accessed from outside and are truly creative in design. The sheet rock has been ripped down in places to reveal rustic brick walls and wooden beams, so that the rooms look like the ruins of some ancient building.

If you are into history, you might do a little research on the First National Bank. Speculation abounds about Bonnie and Clyde's unusual interest in the bank while they bivouacked in nearby Crandall. As you can imagine, banks don't go out of their way to document robberies, so it would be interesting to see if any records exist.

House Tea: First National Lemonade Tea

Hours: (Store) Mon.-Fri. 9-6, Sat. 9-5 (Lunch) Mon.-Sat. 11-2

Location: Corner of Washington and Grove across from the courthouse

Extended Services: Wedding and Baby Showers, Rehearsal Dinners, Children's Dress-Up

Menu

Sandwiches

Chantilly Chicken - Chicken salad served on a croissant

Delightful Deli - Choice of turkey, ham, or roast beef served on whole wheatberry bread, honey mustard, lettuce, tomato, and cheese

Regular Hoagie - Includes turkey, ham, roast beef, honey mustard, lettuce, tomato, and cheese served on a hoagie bun

Special Hoagie - Includes turkey, ham, cream cheese, ripe olives, honey mustard, lettuce, tomato and cheese

All non-herbal tea comes from the
Camellia Sinensis shrub.

Keller

🌀 Cinnamon Sticks

124 South Main Street
817-431-3039
http://www.giftshop-tearoom.com

When the Front Porch res-
taurant closed its doors in
the old railroad town of
Keller, Paul and Peggy Harrison mourned the loss of a
quiet, quaint place to enjoy
a spot of tea and some
lunch. After extensive
travel to England, Wales,
and Germany, the former
engineer and musician
decided that the vacant
1923 farmhouse down the
street would be the perfect
place for a new tearoom,
etcetera.

The "etcetera" part of
Cinnamon Sticks includes a
clock repair shop, a gift
shop, and a pottery painting
shop. Upstairs in the Mad
Platter, guests can "Paint
till you Faint" teapots and other whimsical pottery pieces. The Splendid
Moments Painting Parties offers tea and desserts downstairs and then two
hours of painting classes with artist Debra Johnson, for showers, girl's
night-out parties, or just for grins.

Inside the low-beamed ceilings and wooden floors of the tearoom,
tables are scattered in secluded hall alcoves and in cozy rooms with fireplaces. The bigger rooms are popular for the special holiday theme parties
Cinnamon Sticks offers on Valentine's Day, Mother's Day, and Christmas.

Whenever you choose to visit, don't forget to mention your name to Cleo, the FIC (Feline In Charge), who typically can be found pretending to snooze on a perch in the front herb garden. Cats have connections.

House Tea: Raspberry Spice and Cinnamon Orange Spice

Hours: (Store) Tues.-Sat. 10-4; (Lunch) Tues.-Sat. 11-2; (Tea) by reservation

Location: At the crossroads of FM 1709 and Highway 377

Extended Services: Wedding and Baby Showers, Rehearsal Dinners, Take-out, Pottery Painting

Menu

Salads

Chicken Salad   Fruit Salad
Seafood Salad

Sandwiches

Sliced Turkey and Avocado Sandwich
Smoked Turkey Salad   Seafood Sandwich
Veggie Sandwich   Chicken Salad Sandwich

Entrees

Quiche   Curried Chicken and Fruit Salad

Lake Worth

 ## All Things Country Tearoom

5725 Jacksboro Highway
817-237-3398
http://www.allthingscountry.com

If you have any doubts about the popularity of collectibles, just chat for five minutes with Vivian Martin, the owner of All Things Country. The craft store turned tearoom and collector's heaven has found an untapped niche in the market. Vivian and her daughter, a webmistress extraordinaire, spend the morning returning online inquiries about Harley Davidson, Betty Boop, and Mary Engelbreit licensed collectibles, while manning the Beanie hotline and running a very busy store and tearoom.

The memorabilia have become so popular, in fact, that All Things Country just relocated to a 7,000-square-foot site up the road. Vivian says she needed the extra space just to keep up with the increasing demands of devotees searching for Coca Cola polar bears, John Deere baby tractor banks, and Mary's Moo Moo's square dancing cows.

As you weave your way through the dogs and frogs, teacups, trains, and pterodactyls, the airy country blue tearoom beckons you to the back of the store. Not added until four years after the store's opening, the tearoom has a fan club of its own. For six years the tearoom has been the location of choice for showers and weddings. All Things has become such a favorite haunt for locals, that in the few weeks the new tearoom remained closed for construction, Vivian would find parched guests on her doorstep gasping, "Tea, tea." Never fear, the taps are flowing again, and now All Things enjoys the added benefit of accommodating much bigger group functions.

House Tea: Orange Spice and Cranberry

Hours: (Store) Mon.-Thurs. 10-6, Fri.-Sat. 10-5, Sun. 1-5 (Lunch) Mon.-Sat. 11-3

Location: On the hill across from the radio tower. Note: Jacksboro Highway is also Lake Worth Boulevard and Highway 199.

Extended Services: Wedding and Baby Showers, Rehearsal Dinners, Receptions

Lewisville

When Magnolias Bloom

109 West Main
(Inside The Old Red Tractor Antique Store)
972-420-0026

If the red flower wagon is sitting out front, they are open. Filled with English furniture, quilts, and vintage clothing, the Old Red Tractor Antique Store has lured shoppers to Lewisville for five years. Collectors come for the antiques or the custom-made barbecue sauce, but the younger aficionados know that this is the place for *the* best fudge west of the Mississippi, and probably the east as well. With its old-fashioned candy counter given the People's Choice award for confection affection and its children's tearoom, the Old Red Tractor may be the only antique store in Texas that kids voluntarily visit.

The candy counter is filled with goodies to satisfy tastes both contemporary and purist. Jars filled with red hots, wax lips, swizzle sticks, and root beer barrels fill every horizontal surface. But if you are a true sugar epicurean, try the knock-your-socks-off fudge. Made by hand in a Teflon-coated electric skillet and aluminum bowl, it's just like grandma used to make, or someone's grandma used to make. The flavors range from typical chocolate varieties to the gourmet types, like pumpkin, Brandy Alexander, and ultra rich, which might require a jog to Amarillo to avoid the guilt.

Around the corner from the candy is the When Magnolias Bloom tearoom. Named in honor of the spectacular blossom display the day their son was born, Magnolia's offers children's dress-up tea parties. No minimum number is required so that no guest will have to miss a party due to insufficient headcount. With five boys of their own, owners Cathy and George Huley know what it is like to organize a dozen busy souls with conflicting schedules. This generous allowance has created a boom in their tea party business. Large groups like the Girl Scouts and Daisy Scouts hold their badge functions here, but smaller parties of three, four, and five are very prevalent. Each child goes home stuffed with food, a bit of tea folklore, manners, and a goody bag for later.

House Tea: Strawberry Kiwi and Sugar Plum Spice

Hours: (Store) Tues.-Fri. 11:30-5, Sat. 11-5:30, Sun.-Mon. by reservation. (Religious or allergy restrictions are requested)

Location: Off I-35

Extended Services: Children's Dress-Up

Mabank

 Victorian Lady Tearoom

114 E. Market Street
903-887-1837

If you ask them what is unique about their town, the citizens will tell you it is small and quiet and they like it that way. Only an hour east of Dallas, Mabank has access to the big city with all the small town advantages. Known for its rodeo, which attracts bronco busters and barrel riders from all over Texas, 100-year-old Mabank has experienced a recent resurgence in population, which is due in major part to the united efforts of the town's store owners.

All of the businesses critical for life in a small town line both sides of the restored downtown. The Chamber of Commerce, city hall, and library face the old-fashioned barbershop, jewelry store, toy store, and tearoom. You can take care of your driver's license, return your book, play Nintendo while you get your hair cut, and still have time to pick up an early birthday present for yourself before your retired teacher lunch next door.

The Victorian Lady and the jewelry store is the his and hers project of Janice and Charley Brock. He has been selling jewelry in Mabank for twenty-three years, and she has been running the restaurant for six. The two buildings adjoin, so they can lend each other a hand if needed. Inside, the Victorian Lady is decorated in pink and green with white wrought iron chairs and floral tablecloths. Crystal candleholders sit on each lace overlay that matches the lace curtains.

Save some room for dessert. You won't want to miss the cream cheese pound cake with the strawberries and lemon sauce.

House Tea: Victorian Lady Secret Blend

Hours: Mon.-Fri. 11-2

Location: Downtown

Extended Services: Wedding and Baby Showers, Rehearsal Dinners

Mansfield

 ## Main Street Tearoom

120 N. Main Street
817-473-2977

Sometimes photographs simply don't do justice to the overall cuteness of a place. In downtown Mansfield, the charming Main Street Tearoom is just such a case. Owner Nicole Cawley talked her mother into meticulously marble sponging the cobalt blue walls, which perfectly match the blue and cheerful yellow linens. Sconces with trailing tendrils of morning glory vines line one wall of the narrow tearoom. The opposite wall features a chest-high barn wood picket fence also wrapped in the morning flower. Twinkly lights in the foliage, hurricane lamps, fresh daisies, and salt shakers in the shape of little Victorian girls complete the ensemble.

   Although Main Street now serves breakfast, the folks at the Chamber
of Commerce next door highly recommend the lunch menu's broccoli
cheese soup, almond chicken salad, and the scones, whose cinnamon
aroma tortures them every morning. They've all generously volunteered
as taste-testers. Strawberry Apricot, Peach, and Mango serve as staple
teas, but for the adventurous, try the German potpourri teas that Nicole's
grandparents send over from Deutschland. Die Früchtezauber with rose
hips and hibiscus make a delightful brew either hot or cold, and the Firehouse Chimney tea will make you stand up and say "Achtung."

   While you are out in that neck of the woods, try to catch the hot air balloon festival in June or the Bandana Bash Casino and Auction, where you
can buy the object of your desire for thirty, thirty-five, thirty-five, do I hear
forty? Going once, twice, sold to the lady with the extended pinkie.

House Tea: Strawberry Apricot, Peach, or Apricot Mango

Hours: Mon.-Fri. 7-2:30

Location: Downtown

Extended Services: Wedding and Baby Showers, Rehearsal Dinners,
Catering, Breakfast

Menu

Salads

Almond Chicken Salad - Chicken with toasted almonds, sliced grapes, and celery

Chicken Caesar Salad - Romaine lettuce, Parmesan, olives, croutons, and grilled chicken breast

Tuna Salad - Tuna salad with fruit, poppy seed dressing, lettuce, and tomato

Spaghetti Salad - Marinated pasta with herbs, tomato, and onion

Sandwiches

Almond Chicken Salad - Served with lettuce and tomato on a croissant

Tuna Salad - Served with lettuce and tomato

Club - Lettuce, tomato, turkey, ham, bacon, and cheese melted with mayonnaise

Roast Beef and Swiss - Served with Dijon mustard heated on sourdough bread

Portobella - Lettuce, tomato, purple onion, and pesto mayonnaise on a kaiser roll

Turkey - Turkey, lettuce, tomato, cheese, and mustard on a kaiser roll

Egg Salad - Served with lettuce and tomato

English Breakfast is a blend of Assam, Ceylon, and African.

The best tea grows below 6,000 feet elevation and in 70-80% humidity.

Trained monkeys harvest Monkey Picked Oolong from cliffs too steep for humans.

McKinney

 ## The Muslin Angel

110 S. Tennessee
972-569-8225

The Muslin Angel is not a meeting ground for heavenly hosts. Named for their original business, making Victorian brocade wedding dresses, the store evolved over the years into a tearoom and tea merchant par excellence. With over ninety varieties to choose from, the Muslin Angel is sort of a candy shop of tearooms. The house tea is Buckingham Palace, the blend designed for Queen Elizabeth's spring garden party in honor of people who have made a great contribution to the British Empire. The Chocolate Mint tea makes a great sorbet, and the Cranberry Cooler can be used as a mulling spice for cider. For fruit lovers, there is Watermelon tea or Bellacoola, which smells like Hi-C fruit punch. The Lemon Green tea smells exactly like lemon drops. For the fermentation connoisseur, Amaretto, Piña Colada, Grenadine, and Irish Creme teas are available sans alcohol. With all the variety, you can have a different tea every day without repeating yourself. Buy a little of everything and have a Name That Smell competition before your tea tasting party at home.

The menu at the tearoom is patterned after the Empress in Victoria, an institution in Afternoon Tea. Like the Empress, the Muslin Angel is designed in an antique English look. Green and gold striped wallpaper matches the three-tiered lace and floral tablecloths. The crystal, silver, and china are all authentic, down to the silver Tussie Mussie conversation pieces. These were herbal bouquet holders favored by unhygienic aristocrats in order to endure the proximity of their non-bathing associates—sort of a medieval breath mint. On the tables, sugar comes in all the standard forms but also is available in floral iced sugar cubes and rock candy swizzle sticks.

While you are there, make sure you pick up some of their recipes for cooking with tea. The Orange Spice baked chicken is especially recommended.

House Tea: Buckingham Palace and Chocolate Mint

Hours: (Store) Tues.-Sat. 10ish-5ish; (Tea) Tues.-Sat. 2-4:30

Location: Just off the main square

Extended Services: Wedding and Baby Showers, Rehearsal Dinners, Receptions, Catering, Tea Tastings, Tea Talks, Complete Wedding Arrangements

The Opera House

107 N. Kentucky
972-562-3818

"And coming up the back stretch, it's Four Poster Pete in the lead followed closely by Ted Trundle and Sam Sleighbed. Crossing the finish line, it's Four Poster Pete by a knob!" In September the Harvest Fest and Great McKinney Bed Race box-springs into action for charity. Throughout the weekend mobile mattresses and flying futons drag race around the downtown square while fiddlers saw for the gold nearby. Surrounded by clever knickknack stores filled with Texana, teddy bears, antiques, and garden supplies, the courthouse square hosts a number of events from Mayfair on the Square in summer to a Dickens of a Christmas with live reindeer and Norman Rockwall vignettes in December.

From the west side of the square, the Opera House tearoom has the best seat in town for the festivities. The restored 1800s opera house that once gave John Philip Sousa top billing now feeds the throngs of busy shoppers and festival hoppers.

"Tea, Earl Gray, Hot."

– Captain Jean-Luc Picard,
Stardate 41697.9

Adorned in simple white linens with dark floral place mats and napkins, the tearoom's raised floor bustles with walk-ins while the glassed enclosure provides seating for the abundance of private parties that fill the reservation book.

Do remember to schedule yourself enough time to walk around after lunch. McKinney is the sort of "happening" kind of place that you should take your shop-aholic friends from out of town. Isn't it nice to know that if you get tired, you can hitch a ride on a passing waterbed?

House Tea: Apricot

Hours: Mon.-Sat. 11-3

Location: On the west side of the main square

Extended Services: Wedding and Baby Showers, Rehearsal Dinners, Receptions

Menu

Salads

Chicken Mandarin Salad - Three greens, chicken, vermicelli noodles, Mandarin oranges, water chestnuts, raisins, and sweet basil dressing

Spinach Salad - Turkey, ham, cheese, celery, raisins, apples, and spinach dressing

Crispy Fried Chicken Salad - Served with creamy orange ginger dressing

Bacon, Lettuce, and Tomato Salad - With sweet basil dressing

Stuffed Tomato with White Tuna and Pecans

Stuffed Tomato with Chicken Salad

Sandwiches

Sliced Turkey or Ham with Swiss - Served on a croissant with dill sauce

Country Sandwich - Whole wheat bun with turkey, ham, cheese, lettuce, tomato, green pepper, Vidalia onion, and pickle

Three Layer Reuben - Turkey pastrami, Dijon mustard, sauerkraut, and Swiss cheese

Tuna or Chicken Cheese Melt

Entrees

Vegetable Lasagna - Spinach, carrots, mushrooms, green chili peppers, and noodles

King Ranch Mexican Casserole - White chicken, tortillas, and a creamy cheese and green chili sauce

Chicken Broccoli Crêpes - Creamed broccoli and mushrooms topped with white wine béchamel sauce

Eggplant Lasagna	Spinach Cabrini
Chicken Spaghetti	Chili-Layered Frito Platter

Muenster

Crafty Olde German Tea Haus

216 N. Main
940-759-2519

Guten tag! Wilkommen zu Muenster, population 50,000 during the Germanfest and 1,400 at all other times. One hour from Dallas, this Germanic community with its great shopping is described by natives as one of those "get away from the city kind of places." Muenster's fame stems mostly from its Oktoberfest, which it celebrates in April because the inhabitants "dare to be different." From all over Texas, visitors come to oompah in the Tanz Hall, stagger in the Fun Run, jam to techno-Deutsch rock bands, and stuff their faces with the best of the wurst, compliments of local Fischer's meat market.

If sausage and kraut are not your thing, polka over to the Crafty Olde German Tea Haus for some broccoli grape salad and chocolate Bavarian cream. Tucked away in the family-owned Hoedebecke Marktplatz, Crafty serves both regional delights, like pretzel sandwiches, and gourmet edibles including dazzling desserts.

> "There are few hours in life more agreeable than the hour dedicated to the ceremony known as afternoon tea."
>
> – Henry James

Check out the tower of ice cream, caramel, and drizzled chocolate aptly named Mile High Pie. Crafty sells its own cookbook, but some of the most notorious recipes are intentionally missing to lure you back.

Before you leave, you may want to visit the gift shop to fill in any gaps in your Hummel or Cherished Teddies collection.

House Tea: Apricot

Hours: Mon.-Sat. 11-2

Location: FM 373, Second block on right. Look for the nutcracker on the building.

Extended Services: Wedding and Baby Showers, Rehearsal Dinners, Receptions

North Richland Hills

 The Garden Cottage

5505 Davis Boulevard
(Inside Golightly's Gallery)
817-656-9760

In the back of Golightly's Gallery, home of treasures from
Victorian to shabby chic,
thrives the Garden Cottage, a
sunny patio tearoom run by
the mother and daughter duo
of team Golightly. For fifteen
years, Janet Golightly has
filled North Richland Hills
homes with lovely antiques
and gifts while her children
finished their homework in
the back room. The children
are grown now, but daughter
Jennifer became so fond of
the place, she took over the
management of the tearoom.

Jennifer's love of cooking
adds spark to the menu and
lures the eager locals to try
new delicacies as well as the
golden oldies. The desserts
might be banana caramel pie
or chewy butter cake, but the
Peach Praline hot tea served in a demitasse with a muffin remains their
trademark dish. The lasagna soup and the cream of almond soup were
voted the best picks by most customers, but it was the pumpkin soup that
inspired one lady to have craving dreams. No one is sure as to whether or
not she was pregnant.

House Tea: Peach Praline

Hours: (Store) Mon.-Sat. 10-6, Sun. 1-5; (Lunch) Tues.-Sat. 11-2; (Closed on Sundays during summer)

Location: Off Grapevine Highway 26

Extended Services: Wedding and Baby Showers, Rehearsal Dinners, Children's Dress-Up

Menu

Salads

Texas Bluebonnet Chicken Salad - Chicken, Mandarin oranges, celery, and special seasonings

Garden Gate Salad - Tossed greens and vegetables topped with sunflower seeds

Sandwiches

Wisteria Chicken Salad - Chicken with black olives, celery, and mayonnaise

Canterbury Club - Served on toasted whole wheat with Swiss, cheddar, ham, turkey, and bacon

Tulip Turkey Sandwich   Honeysuckle Ham and Swiss

Entrees

Sunflower Spud   Crepe Myrtle Quiche of the Day

Olney

 ## Magnolia Gold

107 E. Main
940-564-2336

When the days grow short and the sweaters come out of the closet, autumn looms near. The crisp air invigorates the soul, and floating on the breeze wafts the aroma of burning firewood and gunpowder, when you live near Olney, that is, home of the annual One-Arm Dove Hunt. Created by two unilimbed sportsmen, the hunt and subsequent cookout attracts festival-goers to the rural pastures surrounding the town. A wonderful time is had by all, except for the doves, which can probably be found checking the Amtrak tables to Orlando.

If your idea of wild game leans more toward pork tenderloin, make sure you swing by Magnolia Gold tearoom. The garden-muraled walls of this romantic tearoom overlook the wood and glass tables and courtyard decor. Each hunter green (no pun intended) table carries an overlay and napkins in seasonal colors that match the flower arrangements created by the owner herself. The storefront windows of this old clothing store dresses up for the seasons as well. During winter, evergreens with angels and white lights greet the visitor while flowers and spring things celebrate the warmer months. The buttermilk chicken and potato casserole frequent the guest entrees list while the Disappearing Cake, made with chocolate pound cake and chocolate icing, lives up to its name.

If on your way back home you see any waddling feathered hitchhikers, consider offering them a ride. Sometimes they don't have enough bills for the train fare. (Okay, that one was intended.)

House Tea: Peach Apricot

Hours: (Store) Mon.-Fri. 10-5, Sat. 10-2; (Lunch) Tues.-Fri. 11-2

Location: Downtown

Extended Services: Wedding and Baby Showers, Rehearsal Dinners, Receptions

Pantego

Chelsea's Tearoom and Boutique

2421C Park Row
817-276-8100

Each step into Chelsea's is a venture into dress-up wonderland. Feathered boas of every color drape the rooms. Enormous hats, perfect for a day at the Ascot races, pepper the racks of Cinderella dresses. Sequined shoes, tiaras, wedding veils, and costume jewelry await the next tea party. There's even a top hat and cane or two.

Named after the owner's daughter, Chelsea's Tearoom began as a children's clothing boutique. Looking for a way to work and still spend time with her child, Jackie Beagles opened the store and ran it very successfully for several years. When Chelsea was three years old, Jackie had grown

tired of the standard birthday choices of McParties and pizza soirees, so she moved her store and added a tearoom for children.

Now children flock to this popular party spot and dress up like they're going to visit the Queen. After everyone dons her dream wardrobe, the birthday girl is crowned with a special diamond tiara. Once the ladies of leisure enjoy a manicure, they are ready for the parade around the square. Upon retiring to the tearoom, the ladies are versed in etiquette while they eat their crumpets and sip their "tea" from the miniature silver service.

Chelsea's makes the grownup in us say, "Why didn't they have places like this when we were kids?"

House Tea: Lemonade

Hours: Mon.-Fri. 10-6, Sat. 10-5:30, Sun. 12-5

Location: Park Row at Bowen. Note: Pantego is an island in Arlington

Extended Services: Children's Dress-Up

What Americans call "High Tea" is actually an English Low Tea, made of pastries and finger sandwiches. "Afternoon Tea" would be the politically correct term.

Plano

◎ Homemade Delights

1400 Avenue J
(Inside Cobwebs Antique Mall)
972-424-5982

Grab your goggles and your duster jacket, the Mad Hatter Classic Car Club is rolling to Homemade Delights for some white chocolate cheesecake with raspberries. Nestled in the back of Cobwebs Antique Mall in Plano's restored downtown, Delights attracts loads of interesting groups who find the location handy and the food divine. Book clubs, senior citizens groups, and even a china-painting club make this cozy spot their headquarters.

Delights is the quintessential tearoom: a dainty, peppermint-striped haven of embroidered tablecloths, ironed linen napkins, and tea theme decor so cute you'll want to call your grandmother for a lunch date. A tea-cup chandelier suspends over two-tops with mismatched bistro chairs and floral cushions. A tiny teddy bear tea party sits in the center of one of the double handful of lacy tables. A teapot water fountain percolates in the corner. Teapots appear as salt and pepper shakers, bud vases, and in the table lace. Even the owner, Pat Vickery, dons her tea apparel for the occasion.

Whether ordering the chicken salad, the orange crêpes, or the Chicken Divine, the à la king-type dish created for the Easter menu and continued by popular demand, all guests receive the sorbet du jour to cleanse the palate and tiny flowers bedecking their entrees. Then it's on to the second course of soups, including black bean, chilled strawberry, and Italian wedding soup. Don't forget to save room for dessert. Pat brought her experience as a pastry chef to the tearoom and tempts the clientele with her decadent creations. The Heathbar pie and bread pudding with apricot brandy sauce head the permanent dessert list, but come back and try them later if the apple dumplings with cinnamon amaretto sauce or the piña colada cake with strawberries Romanoff and Eagle Brand milk get penciled in. You could hurt yourself.

House Tea: Apricot or Orange Spice

Hours: Mon.-Sat. 11-2:30

Location: Corner of 14th and J Street

Extended Services: Wedding and Baby Showers, Rehearsal Dinners, Catering

Menu

Salads

Chef Salad Bowl - Smoked turkey, ham, Swiss, cheddar, and tomato

Light Crunchy Chicken Salad - Lettuce, broccoli, water chestnuts, tomato, chicken sprinkled with Parmesan, and a light red wine vinegar, soy sauce, and oil dressing

Caesar Salad	Chicken Salad
Egg Salad	Pasta Salad
Garden Salad	Tuna Salad

Sandwiches

Chicken Salad	Egg Salad
Ham and Cheese	Smoked Turkey and Cheese
Tuna Salad	Vegetable

Entrees

Baked Potato - Filled with broccoli-cheese or choice of sour cream, butter, margarine, cheese, chives, and bacon

Quiche - Quiche of the day

🌐 Into My Garden

1017 E. 15th Street
(Inside Nooks and Crannies)
972-509-0292

Softly in the distance a whisky voice croons, "Won't you tell him please to put on some speed, follow my lead, oh, how I need, someone to watch over me." You hope she finds what she's looking for, but you have a cup of Tazo's Zen tea in your hand and you're feeling no pain. If you return tomorrow, you may get Om tea as the apéritif in that delicate porcelain demitasse. After drinking it, you can say deeply profound things about your chicken salad. But today you have escaped from the nearby telecommunications corridor of Richardson and into Nooks and Crannies in downtown Plano for a relaxing lunch.

Past the children's toys, the wedding gifts, the baking section, and the baskets, the wooden floors lead you to the open space of the Into My Garden Tearoom. Fragile beaded vintage shawls drape dramatically from shelves displaying old picture frames, Ascot hats, and other Victorian knickknacks. A cabinet with the owner's personal collection of chintz china stands proudly at the counter, opened only when the elaborate cups and saucers are used for Afternoon Teas. On the white linen tables, the light from pixie lamps flicker off the bent silver forks used as easels. The tiny cards they bear announce the upcoming Afternoon Tea Class discussing menu planning and etiquette.

If you haven't de-stressed yourself by the time you finish lunch, stop by the mood candles on your way out. Next to the black tea and honey candle and the Chai tea oolong sits one marked Revitalization. Take a big whiff and you should be set for five more hours of the work grind.

House Tea: Raspberry or Peach

Hours: Mon.-Sat 11-3:30

Location: Downtown

Extended Services: Wedding and Baby Showers, Rehearsal Dinners, Afternoon Tea, Tea Classes

Menu

Salads

Hearty Caesar Salad - Romaine lettuce tossed with Caesar dressing, Parmesan cheese, and croutons

Wild Chicken and Rice Salad - Blend of herbs and spices topped with cashews

Cold New Orleans Pasta Salad - Marinated chicken and garden vegetables in pasta tossed with a French dressing

Orange Almond Salad - Romaine, sliced scallions, Mandarin oranges with tarragon leaves tossed in tarragon wine vinegar

Chicken Salad Elegant - Roasted chicken breast with grapes and toasted almonds tossed in a creamy herb dressing

Sandwiches

| Tuna Salad | Egg Salad |
| Chicken Salad | Smoked Turkey |

Garden Vegetable - With tomato, onion, avocado, sprouts, and cream cheese

Palm Court

1300 Custer
(Inside Antiqueland Mall)
972-509-7878

Like a superhero, the Palm Court of Plano appears as a mild-mannered tea-room by day but a daring restaurant by night. Nestled in the corner of Antiqueland Mall, the maroon and white tablecloths, floral green carpet, and fresh flowers that seem so perfectly suited to a refined lunch in the bright afternoon, turn intimate by candlelight, when the pimento cheese gives way to pecan chicken.

The guest list changes with the twilight hours also. During the day, antique shoppers, local merchants, and business executives enjoy the lighter repast and the formal English Teas, served with imported goose-berry preserves, banana nut finger sandwiches, and fresh lemon curd for the scones. In the evening, local couples arrange their assignations over the prime tenderloin with peppercorn sauce.

The Palm Court tortures diet-minded visitors by marching them past dessert cases filled with Italian creme cake, cranapple and strawberry rhu-barb pies, and the Chocolate Oblivion Cake, which "you've gotta be a real chocoholic to finish" according to the owners. Cruel, very cruel, but what a way to go.

House Tea: Peach

Hours: (Store) Mon.-Wed. 10-6, Thurs.-Sat. 10-8, Sun. 11-6; (Lunch) Mon.-Sun. 11-2:30; (Dinner) Thurs.-Sat. 5-8; (Tea) Mon.-Sun. 3-5

Location: 15th and Custer

Extended Services: Wedding and Baby Showers, Rehearsal Dinners, Receptions, Catering, Afternoon Tea

Menu

Salads

Chef Salad - With ham, turkey, Swiss cheese, and provolone cheese

Cobb Salad - With rows of chicken, bacon, avocado, egg, and Bleu cheese

Blackened Chicken Caesar Salad - With bacon and tomato croutons

Sandwiches

Palm Court Club Sandwich   Chicken Salad
Philly Cheese Sandwich   Tuna Salad
Bacon, Lettuce, and Tomato   Smoked Turkey
Pimento Cheese   French Dip

Entrees

Quiche of the Day   Chicken Fried Steak
Pecan Chicken   Pot Roast
Casserole of the Day   Fish of the Day

 Tea Time Treasures

1016 E. 15th Street
972-516-8390

Up, up, and away, every year propane enthusiasts blast over J. R. Ewing's shack fifteen miles north of Dallas. From around the country, pilots and their chase crews send their hot air balloons skyward for the annual race that made Plano the Balloon Capital of Texas. Traditionally held in the cow pasture across from Collin County Community College this race takes place in September when the cold, dense autumn air sends the warm gases in the balloon aloft. When the gas cools, the balloon sinks, sometimes into a nearby yard, highway, or lake. The mass ascension starts in the early morning when the calmer air patterns allow the pilots to rise to the air current going in the correct direction. Hundreds of parti-colored Christmas ornaments coast over the houses and highways, causing motorists to pull over and stare. Competitions include speed and distance races and the ever-popular favorite, the Key Race. For the larger ascensions, a car key is attached to the tip of a flagpole. The first pilot to pull the key off gets the new automobile it unlocks.

One of the first stores they fly over is Tea Time Treasures in downtown Plano. Behind the window with the dancing psychedelic teapots, Tea Time offers American Girl Parties for any age. Past the gift shop stocked with cards, tea kits, and scone mixes, wisteria drapes from the ceilings onto an archway trellis. The purple flower motif continues in paint on the walls. White chairs circle tables with cake centerpieces made of satin and ribbons. In the corner a stand holds dozens of vintage hats for the petite guests. For children the menu includes petit fours, finger sandwiches, chocolate soup, fruit, and tea cakes. The adult menu includes cucumber sandwiches, tea breads, fruit salad, and petit fours.

Tea Time often serves as the proving ground for scout manner badges. At any given time thirty-five miniature Ranger Ricks surround the table intensely absorbing the etiquette required for that piece of sewn fabric. You've never seen such a well-behaved group in your life. Emily Post would be proud.

House Tea: Lemonade for kids, Strawberry for adults

Hours: Wed.-Sun. 10-5

Location: Downtown Plano

Extended Services: Wedding and Baby Showers, Children's Dress-Up

Rockwall

 ## Her Secret Garden

1300 Rockwall Pkwy. #102
972-771-5528

Get your kicks on the tiny little stretch of Route 66 in our area. Extending from Garland past the cotton and onion fields flooded to form Lake Ray Hubbard and the novelty stores of Goliad Place, this scenic piece of asphalt Americana abruptly brakes in Greenville. Today, exit in Rockwall, where wit and wisdom get dispensed with the Mister Misties.

Like knights of old, local sages in cowboy hats dispense "information and free advice" from their appointed roundtable at the town's Dairy Queen. These natives will regale you with tales of local intrigue, dispute the origin of the county-long rock wall that gave the town its name, and assure you that their town is absolutely the closest place to Heaven you can mortally get without a prescription. Heading this cast of characters is a ninety-three-year-young gentleman whose wife inspired the dedication of the local school. He says they named the bike rack after him.

Just down the street sits Her Garden Tearoom, an elegant affair overlooking the woods across the street. Enclosed in a semicircle of windows, the maroon and Battenburg lace tables showcase stemmed goblets and miniature topiaries. White lights, grapevine loops, and roses cover the ceiling, and a fountain gurgles in the corner. Of special interest on the menu is the orange-almond salad or the toasted raisin nut bread with ham and cheese. Be sure to save room for the chocolate pound cake.

Her Secret Garden also includes a gift shop that specializes in invitations for weddings and other extravaganzas. A variety of cards cover the tables with topics ranging from gardening to cookouts. Choose from a collection devoted to tea parties, and you'll be ready for your next group excursion.

House Tea: Apricot, Plum, Raspberry, or Strawberry in rotation

Hours: (Store) Tues.-Sat. 10-3; (Lunch) Tues.-Sat. 11-2

Location: Highway 205 near I-30

Extended Services: Wedding and Baby Showers, Rehearsal Dinners, Catering, Children's Dress-Up, Afternoon Tea

Royse City

 ## Victoria's Tearoom

122 E. Main
(Inside Royse City Antique Mall)
972-635-6410

Inside the Royse City Antique Mall lies Victoria's, the rustic and unconventional tearoom that trades its lace and ruffles for homey and historic. The distressed wood paneling of the huge open space bears Jerald "Mr. Royse City" Bailey's tribute to the former businesses of his hometown. This mural, made of ancient fences, wood from the old water tower, and tin from street signs, covers the wall and portrays the story of the town throughout the 1940s and '50s. One room with a long wooden table and barn door cupboards filled with country antique china resembles a farm kitchen so much you can smell the biscuits baking. The scattering of simple white wooden tables and chairs adds a clean, uncluttered look. For those who love the great outdoors, the tearoom extends to a deck with white wrought iron tables and umbrellas. Before you leave, don't forget to find a reason to visit the facilities. The interior decor is quite unusual.

Victoria's presents a full range of interesting events. Fashion shows from a local buyer appear at scheduled intervals. If you like something in particular, the buyer will bring racks of the clothes to your house for private purchasing. At their High Noon Tea Talks, speakers relate historical tidbits about tea to the fascinated audience. The all-time favorite event continues to be the Condensed Storytelling Hour, where the local teller-of-tall-tales spins a *Reader's Digest* version of some poignant novel. Recently, the story of women during the Civil War left audience members crying in the aisles. They were forced to buttress their sorrowful souls with some truly excellent cobbler.

House Tea: Orange Pekoe

Hours: (Store) Mon.-Fri. 11-5, Sat. 11-4; (Lunch) Mon.-Sat. 11-2

Location: Downtown

Extended Services: Wedding and Baby Showers, Rehearsal Dinners, Catering, Afternoon Tea, Storytelling

Menu

Salads

Chef Salad - Turkey, ham, bacon, egg, cheese, tomato, and onion on a bed of lettuce

Southwest Grilled Chicken Salad - Chicken strips, tomato, cheese, olives, and onion on a bed of lettuce

Dinner Salad - Lettuce, tomato, olives, and cheese

Sandwiches

Club Sandwich - Ham, turkey, bacon, American cheese, lettuce, and tomato

Chicken Salad on Croissant   Ham or Turkey on Croissant

Salado

 ## Pink Rose Tearoom

102 N. Main Street
254-947-9110

To be sung to "Rawhide":

Rollin', rollin', rollin',
keep that stagecoach rollin'.
Rollin', rollin', rollin', let's dine.

From Austin to Waco
we need to take a break-o,
Salado is the closest we can find.

Pioneers may not have sung those exact words as they bounced and slammed against the stagecoach walls on their way to Austin. But you can hum along as you zoom down the interstate to the very same rest stop, Salado.

Visionary Col. Elijah Sterling C. Robertson created a college for farmers to excel in the arts, including public speaking, drama, writing, and debating. This practice established the well-educated country folk who now populate the town. The restored main street boasts the artisans and antique dealers who made the town famous in collector circles. Pottery throwers, glass blowers, Highland mavens, and even a hot air balloon maker find their home in this artsy forum.

Among the galleries sit the Rose Cottage Gift Shop and Pink Rose Tearoom. Designed in, you guessed it, pink roses, the tearoom pulses with busy shoppers and tourists catching a bite of lunch. The wooden floors wander through the floral rooms and gift shop brimming with tea paraphernalia and other memorable items.

If you are scoping out a place for a reception or ice cream social, look no further than the backyard enclosed in a whitewashed picket fence. A throwback to the Pollyanna era, the verdant grass serves as a parking lot for strategically placed white vintage bicycles and white iron carriages too scenic for a photographer to ignore.

House Tea: Peach

Hours: Mon.-Sat. 11-2

Location: On the main street

Extended Services: Wedding and Baby Showers, Rehearsal Dinners, Receptions

Menu

Salads

Garden Salad - Light garden salad made from lettuce, crisp vegetables, and tomato

Pasta Salad - Pasta combined with cheese and vegetables with a light basil dressing and served on a bed of lettuce

Chicken Salad - Chicken salad served on a bed of lettuce with vegetables

Chef Salad - Garden greens with ham, turkey, Swiss cheese, and egg

Stuffed Tomato - Tomato stuffed with chicken or tuna salad

Sandwiches

Croissant Sandwich - Choice of ham, turkey, roast beef, or chicken salad served on a croissant with lettuce and tomato

Chicken Salad - Chicken mixed with grapes, almonds, and celery served with lettuce

Tuna Salad - Tuna salad served with lettuce on home baked wheat or white bread

Pimento Cheese - Pimento cheese salad served with lettuce

Smoked Ham - Smoked ham served with lettuce and tomato

Smoked Turkey - Smoked turkey served with lettuce and tomato

Entrees

Baked Potato - Baked potato served with choice of toppings of butter, sour cream, cheese, and bacon bits

Chicken Spaghetti - Chicken and savory sauce with mushrooms and cheese served on spaghetti pasta

Stephenville

Café Trifles

133 W. Washington
254-918-0990

"It's sort of a tearoom, only bigger," one observer commented. True, tea-rooms are typically small, and some of them only have a handful of tables. But others, like Café Trifles, simply have more of a good thing; 8,000 square feet of a good thing.

Carol Gibson and Stormy Armstrong were returning from a catering convention in San Francisco when they decided it was time to take the next big step in their already expansive catering business. They knew of a building in downtown Stephenville that was formerly a Beall's department store. The two friends called the contractor, and the metamorphosis began.

The display windows across the 100-year-old building were removed, and glassed archways took their place. The scrollwork visible through the windows was painted by local artist Darlene Rouse, who also freehanded the grapevine and castle mural to the left of the entrance. The huge show-room floor was partitioned with columns and French doors so the front room could be used for intimate dining and the back room could house the twenty-foot tables needed for groups of 400. The large tables on the second floor hide behind the white balcony rails and curtains and are also used for political fund-raisers, weddings, and proms. The open space to the right of the front room is perfect for a dance floor, a band, or both.

Although the tearoom has added another dimension to the ladies' business, the majority of their time is still devoted to the catering empire they have established. While guests enjoy the Windsor sandwiches and Caribbean salads, the two ladies build wedding high-rises for 300 out of white cake and little plastic people in gowns and tuxedos. It's hard work, but they must enjoy it, because they always meet guests with a genuine smile. Some people thrive on deadlines.

House Tea: Rotates daily

Hours: Mon.-Fri. 7:30-4

Location: On the square

Extended Services: Wedding and Baby Showers, Rehearsal Dinners, Receptions, Catering, Weddings

Menu

Salads

Chef Salad - Bed of greens with turkey, ham, cheeses, black olives, tomato, and peppers

Caesar Salad - Leaf lettuce, croutons, grated Parmesan, and homemade dressing

Chicken Salad - Chicken salad in a tomato cup on a bed of greens

Chicken Caribbean Salad - Grilled chicken strips with pineapple, pico de gallo, and guacamole on a bed of greens

Pasta Salad - Pasta, celery, olives, and peppers with a vinegar and oil dressing

Santa Fe Chef Salad - Grilled chicken on a bed of greens with corn salsa, cheese, tomato, and guacamole

Sandwiches

Classic Sandwich - Swiss or American cheese, roast beef, pimento, turkey, ham, tuna or chicken salad

Windsor - Turkey, pico de gallo, pineapple, and lettuce on a croissant

Arizona Club - Turkey, bacon, lettuce, tomato, and guacamole on a croissant

Grilled Chicken Sandwich - Served on a bun with lettuce and tomato

Farmers Market Wrap - Served on an herb flavored hand-stretched tortilla wrap with lettuce, tomato, bell pepper, black olives, and sprouts

Southwest Roll Ups - Two hand-stretched flour tortillas served with spicy mustard, lettuce, guacamole, turkey, and pico de gallo

Club Wrap - Bacon, turkey, ham, lettuce, and tomato on an herb-flavored tortilla

Baja Chicken Sandwich - Grilled chicken breast topped with guacamole, lettuce, and tomato

California Club - Grilled chicken, bacon, lettuce, tomato, and guacamole

Chicken Caesar Sandwich - A traditional Caesar salad with grilled chicken breast

Entrees

Veggie Burger - A vegetable patty with lettuce, tomato, and cheese on a kaiser roll

Temple

Carrousel Gift and Judy's Tearoom

1610 S. 31st Street
254-771-3946

In September indulge yourself and that big little boy in your life with a trip to Temple for the Texas Train Festival. Guests can don their overalls and striped caps and watch the steam locomotives, restored Pullman cars, WWII troop sleepers, and new Amtrak cars chug into town. Ride the overgrown model train or peruse the old photos and hand-drawn turn-of-the-century rail blueprints discovered on a false wall of the depot during recent renovations. The gadget-minded can catch the telegraph exhibit or the train tracking board that follows every engine moving in the system.

For the country-at-heart, stick around for the Texas Early Days Tractor and Engine Association Festival where perfectly maintained vintage reepers, binders, threshers, and cotton gins bash and thrash their crop into cash. Poppin' Johns and monster combines snort and swallow side by side to demonstrate how the farmers' lot in life improved over the century. It's hard to imagine that once upon a time exhausted farmers threshed their shocks manually with canes. The chaff blew out the barn door, but the seed remained behind a strategically placed bump on the floor, still called the "threshold." See, now you are ready for the Final Jeopardy round.

To wash the dust from your throat, pop around the corner to Carrousel Gift and Judy's Tearoom for a big gulp of Raspberry tea and desserts voted by *Reader's Choice* as the best in Bell County three years running. Primarily known for their specialty gifts, including Arthur Court engravables, Baltic Sea amber, smocked picture frames, Russian jewelry, wedding dainties, and baby doo-dads, Judy's lures browsers with their choice selection for the person who has everything, but keeps them with a menu for the person who has hunger.

Stuffed tomatoes and cool pasta salads in the summer rotate with heavier dishes for winter. Customers devour the caramel brownies and cranapple pie on vintage china, and the hot teas direct from England taste better because they are served in antique teacups. The mauve and green tables sport Pimpernel English place mats amid the rose and lace decor, and soft instrumental music whispers overhead. For customers who covet the place mats or any of the decor, which apparently happens frequently, they will be delighted to find it all for sale in the gift shop for tea parties of their very own.

House Tea: Raspberry

Hours: (Store) Mon.-Fri. 10-5:30, Sat. 10-4; (Lunch) Mon.-Sat. 10-4

Location: At Avenue R. Two blocks from Scott and White Hospital

Extended Services: Wedding and Baby Showers, Rehearsal Dinners, Receptions

Menu

Salads

Garden Salad	Fruit Salad
Chef Salad	Judy's Salad

Sandwiches

Pimento Cheese	Turkey and Cheese
Ham and Cheese	Chicken Salad
Tuna Salad	Veggie Melt

Van Alstyne

Durning House

205 W. Stephens
903-482-5188
http://www.durninghouse.com

Just outside Sherman, named after Sidney "Remember the Alamo" Sherman, the little town of Van Alstyne presents a whirling kaleidoscope of a tearoom in country colors. The green and barn red Victorian belonged to the Durning family since its construction in 1905, and in typical country-practical fashion, the new owners simply kept the name. Two bed and breakfasts were eventually added in the adjoining buildings, but when they

ran out of space, the owners bought the two-story arts and crafts style house next door for the gift shop.

Inside the main building of the Durning House, the eyes wander over the busy country decor that featured in a recent edition of *Country Decorating Ideas* magazine. The intentionally mismatched china, silver, and glassware happily lounge on a hodgepodge of brocade, lace, floral, and striped tablecloths. One room whirrs with whirligigs—washing clothes, sawing logs, and chopping wood from every spare corner. The back room supports a huge eighteen-wheeler truck grill that covers the wall. Against the opposite wall sit antique gas tanks. The owners tell everyone that the truck got stuck on the way to the pumps.

At night the dim rooms calm to a serene flicker. Crystal candelabras cast romantic shadows during the popular candlelight dinners when the menu expands to more elegant cuisine. If you don't want to drive back after dinner, see if they have any openings at the B&B. Decorated in country antiques, the comfortable rooms will send you off into peaceful fields of dreams.

House Tea: Raspberry

Hours: Tues.-Fri. 11-2, Fri.-Sat. 6-9 P.M.

Location: Six blocks from Highway 75

Extended Services: Wedding and Baby Showers, Rehearsal Dinners, Bed and Breakfast, Candlelight Dinners

Waco

Honey-B-Ham Backyard Café

213 Main Street
(Inside River Square Center)
254-752-7821

In the heart of Waco's revitalized warehouse district sits the River Square Center, a true shopping treasure. This two-story 1890s warehouse, with its high ceilings and creaky wooden staircase, fairly bulges with fascinating novelties. No walls divide the huge open space, so you can browse from one section to the next without interruption. Around the corner from the pet boutique is a children's clothes section that features infant Dallas Cowboy cheerleader uniforms, complete with miniature pom-poms. In the rustic furniture section you can get a bedroom suite and matching chandelier made of antlers to put in your ranch house. Stock up on soap that resembles geodes and metal sculptures of dogs in turtleneck sweaters coasting on sleds. This is the place to get a present for that person who has pretty close to everything.

The Honey-B-Ham Backyard Café rests at the back of the second floor. Appropriately named, this tearoom looks much like the backyard of a farm. The distressed barn wood tables would evoke an Amish aura if not for the imaginative chairs surrounding them. Battle-scarred farm windows, sans glass, suspend by raffia from the ceiling far overhead. They separate the visual space between the tables. Old tricycles and Radio Flyer wagons are parked around the area, just in case you want to take a spin after lunch.

As the name implies, the specialty of the house is Honey-B-Ham and can be shipped for holidays or catered for all occasions. Owner Sharon Barr originally ran multiple Honey-B-Ham Delis in Lewisville and Colleyville with her husband. The huge volume and fast pace of the stores, while desirable, restricted leisurely conversations with the customers. In an attempt to downshift, she took over the Backyard Café. Now she enjoys getting to know her visitors and enticing them to try a new dessert. Remember, if you are indecisive about trying the pumpkin cheesecake or any of the other sinful choices, you can always run up and down the stairs several times after lunch. Before you leave, however, don't forget to take a look out the back windows at the view of the river.

House Tea: Peach and Raspberry

Hours: Mon.-Sat. 10-4

Location: 3rd and Franklin

Extended Services: Wedding and Baby Showers, Rehearsal Dinners, Catering, Box Lunches

Menu

Salads

House Salad - With ham, turkey, lettuce, tomato, carrots, celery, green pepper, radishes, cheese, and croutons

Dinner Salad - With lettuce, tomato, cucumber, carrots, celery, green pepper, radishes, cheese, and croutons

Sandwiches

Honey-B Ham and Cheese - Served with lettuce, tomato, and pickles

Smoked Turkey Breast and Cheese - Served with lettuce, tomato, and pickles

Honey-B Soft Taco, Ham and Turkey - Served with sour cream, guacamole, cheddar cheese, lettuce, and tomato rolled in a flour tortilla

Club Sandwich - Served with ham, turkey, bacon, lettuce, tomato, pickle, and cheese

Ham Salad Sandwich	BLT
Chicken Salad Sandwich	Tuna Salad Sandwich
Chip-Beef Bar-B-Q on Bun	Croissant, Ham and Turkey and Cheese

Entrees

Stuffed Baked Potato - Served with butter and sour cream

The Works - Baked potato with butter, sour cream, cheese, chives, and bacon bits

House Baked Potato - Served with butter, sour cream, cheese, chives, bacon bits, ham, and turkey

The Cowboy - Baked potato with butter, cheese, and chili

Texas Baked Potato - Served with butter, cheese, and barbecue

 The Showroom Café

7524 Bosque, Suite Q
254-772-0720

Of all the tearoom origins, the Showroom Café must surely have the most unusual. Originally, Ron and Nancy Reynolds decided to leave their construction and medical transcription jobs and create a kitchen and bath showroom in Waco. In their store, customers could browse through the fully functioning kitchen layouts and get ideas for their own house design. Because the kitchens included functional appliances, the Reynolds decided to include presentations on storage and cooking and give samples of the gastronomic goodies. These demonstrations became very popular and quickly led to cooking shows and classes.

One Saturday afternoon, a food writer from the *Waco Tribune Herald* attended the Dinners with a Flair presentation and wrote an article about the Showroom's cooking classes. So much interest was generated by this article, that people asked the Reynolds to cater special events with the excellent recipes that were taught. Reynolds Design Catering quickly led to the Showroom Café. After all, they had the kitchens, recipes, multiple dining room sets, and even an excellent reputation for their cuisine.

The Showroom Café now operates as a restaurant as well as a catering business. If you have the food catered, though, you will miss the lovely atmosphere of the café itself. Peppered with antiques and art, the café, as a visiting nine-year-old put it, "feels just like home."

House Tea: Raspberry

Hours: Mon.-Fri. 11-2, Fri.-Sat. 5 P.M.-9 P.M.

Location: Exit Highway 6 off I-35

Extended Services: Wedding and Baby Showers, Rehearsal Dinners, Catering, Children's Dress-Up

Menu

Salads

Garden Salad   Chef Salad
Spring Salad   Greek Salad
Grilled Chicken Salad

Sandwiches

Honey Baked Ham and Cheese - Grilled or cold

Italian Hoagie - With ham, salami, provolone and Swiss, lettuce, tomato, and onion

Grilled Chicken Hoagie - Grilled chicken and Swiss cheese on hoagie topped with grilled veggies, lettuce, tomato, and herb sauce

Grilled Veggie Sandwich - Sautéed veggies and Swiss cheese

Grilled Asparagus Sandwich - Ham or turkey and Swiss with sautéed asparagus and tomato

Chicken Salad Sandwich

Mesquite Smoked Turkey and Cheese

Entrees

Chicken Pasta Toss   Quiche
Marsala Chicken   Chicken and Asparagus Bundle
Beef Tips
Marinated Grilled Chicken Breast with Herb Mashed Potatoes

Walnut Springs

 ## Back Side of Nowhere Tearoom

Third Street (Highway 144)
(Inside the Cottage Boutique)
254-797-8201

Ah, summer, the season when a young man's fancy turns to...rattle-snakes. Coincidentally, you can get your diamondback fix at the annual Rattlesnake Roundup in Walnut Springs, just outside of Glen Rose. Watch the slithering parade or the Rattle Rustle, or volunteer for the daredevil show where brave souls shimmy into a sleeping bag with twenty of their closest serpentine friends. When you've had enough chicken-fried snake tenders, visit the Back Side of Nowhere Tearoom downtown for some non-reptilian lunch and a good ghost story.

Multiple guests have reported smelling flowers near the old embalming room of this 100-year-old former funeral home. Fogs in the tall, vaulted halls, chilling temperatures in summer, and huge candles rolling off tables without provocation have been witnessed by many guests. Owners Kay and John Moore say they have made an agreement with the ghosts that if nothing bothered their guests during the day, then the spirits would be left undisturbed at night.

Fortunately, that leaves plenty of time to enjoy Kay's famous pies. The lemon, chocolate, and coconut meringues are huge, and the Kentucky Derby pie, filled with chocolate chips and pecans, is positively sinful. Just make sure you get out of there by nightfall.

House Tea: Peach

Hours: (Store) Tues.-Sat. 9-5; (Lunch) Mon.-Sat. 11-2

Location: Downtown

Extended Services: Wedding and Baby Showers, Rehearsal Dinners, Children's Dress-Up

> Tea leaves float. So a true teapot should
> have its spout jutting from the bottom of
> the pot. A coffee pot should have its spout
> from the top since the grounds sink.

Waxahachie

🍽 Chantilly Place

311½ South Rogers Street
972-923-0770

Are you going to Scarborough Fair? If so, it would be sage to find thyme to visit Waxahachie, home of the Renaissance Festival for over twenty years. Drag out those broad swords and chain mail bikinis and blend in with the Ren-natives. Tap the King's private kegs during the Royal Ale Festival, cheer for your favorite knight, or participate in the annual wooing competition. If you didn't join the turkey leg eating contest, go in singlets and doublets to Chantilly Place.

Located in a downtown strip of pre-1900s mercantiles, Chantilly has an enormous storefront window with tables where guests can dine and do their mannequin impression. The interior is done in mauves and maroons with rose buds stenciled along the ceiling and lace swags partitioning the tables. Chantilly is the local hangout for lunch. Many of the same folk have eaten here every day for years. They say they come for the stuffed spud soup, but don't be fooled. It's the homemade blackberry and peach cobbler they're after.

Before galloping out of town, check out some of the Queen Anne, Gothic Revival, and Victorian Gingerbread houses for which Waxahachie is famous. It is the "Gingerbread City" after all.

House Tea: Black Current and Tropical

Hours: Mon.-Sat. 11-2:30

Location: 1½ blocks south of the courthouse

Extended Services: Wedding and Baby Showers, Rehearsal Dinners

Menu

Salads

Spinach Salad - Spinach with almonds, Mandarin oranges, and hot bacon dressing

Caesar Salad - Romaine lettuce garnished with almonds, Mandarin oranges, seasoned croutons, and grated Parmesan cheese

Chicken Salad - Served with sliced almonds, Mandarin oranges, and grapes

Sandwiches

Chicken Salad Sandwich - Made with Mandarin oranges, almonds, grapes, and a special dressing on a croissant

Tuna Salad Sandwich - Served on a croissant with lettuce and tomato

Ham and Swiss - Shaved country ham and Swiss cheese with mayonnaise, lettuce, and tomato on a croissant

Shaved Smoked Turkey - Roasted turkey with provolone cheese and mayonnaise, lettuce, and tomato on a croissant

Gourmet Wrapper - Special wrapper filled with turkey, spinach, tomato, cheese, red onion, bell pepper, and black olives

Vegetarian Wrapper - A gourmet wrapper filled with spinach, tomato, cheese, red onion, bell pepper, and black olives

Wichita Falls

 Secret Garden Tearoom

615 Ohio
(Inside Somewhere in Time Antiques)
940-767-5570
http://www.wichitafallsantiques.com/somewhere

The Secret Garden in Wichita Falls is so secret that it cannot be found on 8th Street at all. That is because it just moved to its new location on Ohio Street. The huge 1908 building in which it now resides along with

Somewhere in Time Antiques was originally two adjacent hotels, the Denver and the Dempsey. It was then converted into a hardware store that lasted for fifty years and then into today's antique store and tearoom. Owners Diane Walser and Barbara Douglas saw past the wreckage that the hardware store inflicted on the building and envisioned the beauty that once was there. Even they were surprised when the heavy, utilitarian shelves came down and the vaulted arch doorways, elaborate wainscoting, and lovely architectural touches that had been hiding all of these years were revealed.

Besides looks and space, this new building has the added luxury of a ground floor location. The steep stairs of the tearoom in the previous building made accessibility very difficult for those customers who were not jackrabbits. Now tearoom fans can stroll or roll right across the wooden floors and through the vaulted doorway that once was the hotel's dining room entrance.

The tearoom itself is a clever combination of the stylish and the rustic. The dark green walls and dimmed interior lights emphasize the white lights, oil paintings in gilt frames, and brass ceiling fans. On one of the walls is the facade of an old Victorian house with a weathered wooden porch covered by climbing roses and a door that makes you want to knock to see who answers.

If you picked the right day and were clever enough to make reservations for this busy tearoom, you will be rewarded by live Romantic Saturday Afternoon music as you munch on your Glorious Morning muffins and sip your Plum tea. Otherwise, you will likely be standing in the doorway a long time looking vaguely like a cocker spaniel at dinnertime. The Secret Garden is a very popular niche.

House Tea: Plum or Strawberry

Hours: Mon.-Sat. 11-2

Location: Downtown

Extended Services: Wedding and Baby Showers, Rehearsal Dinners, Catering

"And he sang as he watched
and waited till his billy boiled,
'You'll come a-waltzing
Matilda with me.'"

– from "Waltzing Matilda"

Menu

Salads

Chef Salad - Bed of lettuce with bacon, turkey, ham, cheddar and Swiss cheeses, tomato, cucumber, and pepper Parmesan dressing

Almond Chicken Salad - Tender chunks of chicken mixed with toasted almonds, sliced grapes, Mandarin oranges, crisp celery, and honey mustard dressing

Caesar Salad - Romaine lettuce, Parmesan cheese, croutons, and traditional dressing

Sandwiches

Pepper Turkey Delight - Peppered turkey, cheddar cheese, lettuce, tomato, and honey mustard dressing

Vegetable Pita Pocket - Lettuce, cucumber, tomato, cheddar cheese, and black olives with special dressing served in pita bread

The Garden Club - Shaved turkey breast, crisp bacon, Swiss and cheddar cheeses, lettuce, and tomato

Ham and Swiss Melt - Shaved ham, Swiss cheese, and tomato on toasted sourdough bread

Almond Chicken Salad - Almond chicken salad with lettuce and tomato on a croissant

Tuna Salad - Tuna salad served on wheat bread

French Dip - Roast beef and provolone cheese served on a hoagie roll with au jus

Entrees

Chicken Mushroom Crêpes - Tender chicken and button mushrooms hand rolled in crêpe with a white wine sauce drizzled on top

Elegant Quiche - Prepared in a flaky crust with garden vegetables

Lemon Peppered Chicken Breast - Served over angel hair pasta with a white wine sauce

Northeast

Have Cup Will Travel

Just because some of our American restaurants practice tea bigotry, does not mean you have to stoop to a mug o' the dreaded bean. Take a traveling tearoom with you, and you'll never be caught at teatime without that life-saving caffeine.

Start with a container with a handle. A lunch box will do, but a small Victorian-esque hatbox fits the bill perfectly. Remember to get one little enough to carry into restaurants. Select a favorite cup and saucer and place in the center of the hatbox. Scouring the antique malls for the perfect cup can take some time, but don't buckle until you find one that leaps off the shelf and demands to be taken home, figuratively, that is.

Add the necessary accouterments. Find a home for the sugar, faux-sugar, lemon, and honey first, as a true connoisseur will probably need a shoehorn to stuff just one more tea variety in the case. Take-out packages of sugar and honey fit, but consider splurging on decorator sugar cubes or miniature honey bears to add a touch of panache.

Add a circle of tea bags of your choice. Consider individually wrapped varieties to make identification possible later unless serendipity is your thing. For purists, an assortment of loose tea and a strainer can be substituted for the bags. Pick two or three of each kind or more for the type you drink the most and can get the least, like decaffeinated Earl Grey. Attach a teaspoon with Velcro to the lid. You can create a holster or sleeping cap for it if you feel creative.

Cover the arrangement with a neatly pressed linen napkin and close the lid. Put it in your car for any future expeditions. The next time you ask the waiter if they have herbal tea and he looks at you like you just grew a second head, whip out your traveling house of civility and coolly request hot water. You'll only embarrass your friends the first time. After that, they'll just tell the people at the next table you're actually an eccentric Brit with a Texas twang.

145

Athens

Garden of Eatin'
419 N. Prairieville
903-677-3315

Next door to the Wayward Possum and across from Hog Heaven Hams in Athens is the Garden of Eatin', where the "pies of Texas are upon you." Situated in a former chocolate factory, the Garden still sells truffles as well as gourmet coffee beans and estate sale finds in the adjoining store. The walls are painted with a touch of humor by Trini Blanton, the building's owner. The bricks are painted to resemble stones and the stones are painted like brick walls. The doors on the side of the building lead to the old dock. Candy would be loaded out those doors onto train cars that ran past the building.

The tables of the tearoom are covered with hand embroidered linens, made by a handful of local customers. The furniture comes from Athen's Alley, the antique store across the street. When the Alley runs out of space to store them, they loan the furniture to the tearoom. If you particularly like a chair, feel free to buy it.

The menu changes with a swipe of an eraser as it is written on a chalkboard. The Garden specializes in muffins, chicken salad made with baked chicken, and most especially, pies. The pecans, apples, blueberries, and peaches are all grown by local farmers as are the tomatoes, which are lovingly raised in a greenhouse by a customer of the Garden. If you are very lucky, you may even get some in January.

House Tea: Peach, Apricot, and Raspberry

Hours: (Store) Mon.-Sat. 10-5; (Lunch) Mon.-Sat. 11-3

Location: Three blocks from the square

Extended Services: Wedding and Baby Showers, Rehearsal Dinners, Candy

Big Sandy

Annie Potter's Victorian Village Tearoom

107 N. Tyler
903-636-4952

The Ashley Phelps house in Big Sandy sits among the pine trees on Highway 155 across from the needlework shop and the bed and breakfast. The graceful 1905 Queen Anne and Colonial Revival house that now boasts Annie Potter's Victorian Village Tearoom was originally a boardinghouse for schoolteachers run by Ruth Phelps.

The Wedgwood blue and white trimmed house has a wraparound porch that overlooks the four-foot-high lavender rhododendron and the reflecting pool. Stepping stones lead you past the water fountain, the benches under the huge oaks, and to the little gingerbread playhouse in the back. A duplicate of the big house painted in pink, this adorable little hideaway has two floors and multiple rooms with a staircase and shuttered windows.

Although the tearoom in the big house is dressed with genteel high-backed chairs, burgundy and lace tablecloths, and rose cut glass tea lights, one is definitely tempted to take their tea upstairs in the playhouse instead. Maybe the waitresses can hand your food in through the windows if they know the secret password.

House Tea: Spice Cranberry

Hours: Mon.-Thurs. 11-3, Fri. 11-9, Sat. 8-9 P.M., Sun. 8-3

Location: On Highway 155 North

Extended Services: Wedding and Baby Showers, Rehearsal Dinners, Receptions

Emory

 ## In the Garden Tearoom

114 S. Texas Street
903-473-0948

Every winter the American bald eagles migrate from their aeries in Alaska to nest in the highest perches of Texas. For thirty-four days, the mated pair takes turns warming the eggs. Hatchlings are ready to leave the nest in thirteen weeks. Over the rivers and tributaries of a handful of privileged locales, spectators watch in wonder as the eaglets learn to fly well enough to endure the long journey back to Alaska for the fish spawning season. The town of Emory celebrates their feathered immigrants each January with the Eagle Fest. Tourists travel from all over the country to watch the aerial training lessons and to accept Emory's hospitality.

In the Garden Tearoom enjoys the status as one of the most frequented spots in town. The Victorian restaurant, dressed in mauve, green,
and burgundy, inhabits an old sweet potato house and delights its guests
with secret recipe tea and excellent cuisine. The Rose Room, with its delicate floral entwined lattice and spindle-back chairs, serves as the local
party room and stays booked year round.

If you haven't had your fill of bird watching, travel the few miles to
Wills Point, the Bluebird Capital of Texas. Thousands of Eastern bluebirds
converge on the bricked streets of this little country town like a nonviolent
version of a Hitchcock movie.

House Tea: Special Recipe

Hours: Mon.-Fri. 8:30-2, every third Saturday of the month 11-2

Location: Highway 69 and Highway 19

Extended Services: Wedding and Baby Showers, Rehearsal Dinners

> "Drinking tea on a regular basis may help
> reduce your risk of stroke."
>
> – Better Homes and Gardens, July 1996

Gilmer

 Gazebeaux

203 Tyler Street
903-843-2466

Along the beautiful winding road of Route 155, past the groves of pine trees, wildflowers, and staring cows, lies the sleepy town of Gilmer and the Gazebeaux. This unusual combination of tearoom and lace shop is perfectly situated in the downtown square across from the courthouse. The 1900s brick building in which it resides once housed a Masonic lodge, a bank, and a department store in its long history. Today the front of the building sells the largest collection of Heritage Lace in East Texas. It acts as a showcase shop with over eighteen patterns of lace hanging from every corner available. Table runners with teapots or lighthouses, black lace shawls, and holiday place mats all find their home here.

Community ladies and business people who want to impress their clients frequent the Gazebeaux tearoom in the back of the store. The tables have an undercloth of black to show off the lace place mats and glowing tea lights. The food, like the name, reflects the Louisiana origin of the owners with the tamer spices preferred by local palates. The Garden District Chicken Salad Pie is chicken salad baked in a crust, and the French Quarter Special is whatever the chef feels like whipping up for the day.

Before you leave you can buy a jar of the Jezebel sauce, the secret recipe concoction served with cream cheese and crackers at the table. The owners won't tell you what's in it, so you'll just have to eat enough of it to guess.

House Tea: Raspberry

Hours: Tues.-Sat. 10-5

Location: On the square

Extended Services: Wedding and Baby Showers, Rehearsal Dinners, Receptions, Catering

Menu

Salads

Gazebeaux Grilled Chicken Salad - Grilled chicken breast, sliced and served over salad greens with tomato, shredded carrot, black olives, cheese, sliced egg, bacon, and croutons

Sandwiches

Gazebeaux Chicken Salad Sandwich - Served on toasted white or wheat bread with lettuce, tomato, chips, and fruit garnish

Turkey Sandwich Gazebeaux - Turkey breast served on toasted white or wheat bread with lettuce, tomato, and cheese

Entrees

Louisiana Bayou Pie - Quiche reminiscent of South Louisiana featuring ham, cheese, and grits

Garden District Chicken Salad Pie - Chicken salad baked in a flaky crust

Never swallow medicines with tea. Some
of the chemical compounds may interact
negatively with certain drugs.

Greenville

Generations

4411 Moulton
903-454-6029

Autumn traditionally brings harvest celebrations and no less in Greenville, one of the largest cotton producers in Texas. The Cotton Jubilee held each year in October commemorates the cash crop that once covered the downtown in fluffy snow and still brings billions of dollars of revenue into the state. Beware, anti-polyester laws will be strictly enforced.

When your mouth is so dry you could spit dust, visit Generations for a kidney buster of Snickerdoodle tea. Aptly named for the four generations of Snider women who run it, this tearoom surrounds the guest with country themed decor. A table in bright sunflowers shares floor space with the strawberry table, and old-fashioned kitchen utensils dot the walls. If you order the broccoli salad and the signature chicken salad, maybe you won't feel guilty about the huge slab of toasted coconut caramel pecan pie sauntering your direction.

Before you leave town you might want to check out the American Cotton Museum, which displays historic memorabilia year round and teaches the art of bailing, spinning, and weaving. Take notes, there may be a pop quiz afterward.

House Tea: Raspberry, Cranberry Cream, or Snickerdoodle in rotation

Hours: Mon.-Fri. 11-2

Location: Moulton and Stanford

Extended Services: Wedding and Baby Showers, Rehearsal Dinners, Catering, Children's Dress-Up

 Treasures

2814 Terrell Road
903-455-7736

Greenville keeps a secret treasure just off the main drag. The romantic little tearoom, named Treasures, delights the taste buds and soothes the soul. From overhead, inspirational music flutters across the double handful of lace-dressed tables. Tapestries of thatched cottages and hollyhock gardens warm the eye, and tiny topiary roses make the air a fragrant bower.

Treasures' specialty of the house is the baked potato soup, which is so popular it probably has its own web page by now. Other menu essentials include the chicken salad, the raspberry tart, and the Nieman Marcus cake, which contains "everything wonderful." Certainly cheesecake, custard, and pound cake head the list of ingredients. For folks who want their cake and to eat it too, try the Banana Split cake—vanilla pudding, Cool Whip, bananas, chocolate pudding, and strawberry pie filling with a pecan sandy crust. The chocolate syrup and nuts are added just for artistic effect, of course. The owner, Debra Hager, boasts that you will leave filled. This probably constitutes a vast understatement on her part.

> The higher in elevation the tea plant grows, the lighter the tea.

House Tea: Raspberry Rose

Hours: (Store) Mon.-Sat. 10-5; (Lunch) Mon.-Fri. 11-2

Location: Off the main drag

Extended Services: Wedding and Baby Showers, Rehearsal Dinners, Receptions, Catering, Children's Dress-Up

 **Wesley House**

2208 Wesley Street
888-231-1272
http://www.wesleyhouse.com

The secret is out, Wednesday means "Bubba day" at the Wesley House. Originally, the local attorneys who loved the food at the charming Painted Lady didn't want anyone to see them dining in the ultra fru-fru ambiance. They parked around the corner and darted upstairs to their favorite room. If anyone at their offices asked, they simply told them they were "going to Bubba's." The tearoom now serves heartier dishes and more generous portions on Wednesday in their honor.

Just a hop outside Dallas, the slate gray Victorian with the wraparound porch and oval windows served as a doctor's home and practice in the late 1800s and again in the 1930s. You can still see the two front doors that separated the living quarters from the office. During World War II it was divided into apartments for the field training personnel at Major's Air Force Base. Years later the new owner converted it back to the graceful splendor that now houses a gift shop, clothing boutique, antique corner, and tearoom. Inside, the original rose globe chandeliers suspend over the knotty pine floors and massive oak fireplaces. Upstairs in the tearoom, the lace-covered oversized windows look down on the lawn and garden. White linens with fresh miniature roses and honeysuckle match the period wallpaper. French doors with authentic wavy glass panes visually divide the rooms.

Only three items on the menu remain constant: the chicken salad, three-cheese quiche, and chicken poppy seed. All else changes daily. Specials have included Cornish game hen with warm spinach salad and three-cheese mashed potatoes, or pork medallions in mustard sauce with caramelized green beans and new potatoes with lemon. The desserts range from pies and cobblers to bread puddings and cheesecakes, but for the serious chocolate lover try the baked fudge, served hot and gooey with ice cream. Ouch!

On your way out to your fitness club, look down at the sidewalk leading to the front porch. It was made of ballast stone that Galveston ships used to keep themselves upright after emptying a load of the local cotton in England.

House Tea: Apricot Mango, Passionfruit, or Cherry Berry in rotation

Hours: (Store) Tues.-Fri. 10-6, Sat. 10-5; (Lunch) Tues.-Sat. 11-2

Location: Downtown

Extended Services: Wedding and Baby Showers, Rehearsal Dinners, Catering, Children's Dress-Up

Henderson

 Taste of East Texas

105 E. Main Street
(Inside Main Street Gallery)
903-657-0065

Bring your naked waffles and lonely pancakes to the Main Street city of Henderson for their annual syrup festival. Held in honor of the ribbon cane syrup produced next door in Cushing, the event gives the natives in town a chance to let their hair down and satisfy their collective sweet tooth. You know the local dentists must look forward to this event all year.

Another place to fulfill those carbohydrate dreams is the Taste of East Texas. Tucked in the back of an 1885 former mercantile building still owned after a century by the Alford family, the tearoom lures innocent bystanders off the streets with visions of cheesecakes and decadent chocolate confections. To justify dessert, balance the calories with one of their designer salads, like the chicken oriental or the seafood salad with shrimp and crab. Remember, one bite of lettuce equalizes two bites of cheesecake.

The mauve tables and green oaken chairs of the tearoom extend across the sunken wooden floor at the back of the Main Street Gallery. Wooden banister legs visually separate the dining area from the gift shop and give an air of privacy to the tourists and clubs that prefer to meet there. After lunch you can mosey through the gallery and snoop through the bridal registry shelves. These racks at the front of the store contain the items wedding-goers have purchased off the bride's wish list. Each shelf is labeled with the couple's name and picture from the newspaper. For your best chortle of the day, check out what the local missus-to-be considers indispensable for the well-stocked house.

House Tea: Tropical Breeze

Hours: (Store) Mon.-Sat. 10-3; (Lunch) Mon.-Sat. 11-3

Location: Downtown

Extended Services: Wedding and Baby Showers, Rehearsal Dinners, Catering, Takeout

Menu

Salads

Chicken Oriental Salad - Mixed greens topped with grilled chicken, cheese, cucumber, tomato, and oriental noodles topped with honey mustard dressing

Chef Salad - Mixed greens topped with ham, turkey, cheese, tomato, hard-boiled egg, and purple onion

Seafood Salad - Mixed greens topped with shrimp, crab, avocado, alfalfa sprouts, tomato, and purple onion

Dinner Salad - Mixed greens, tomato, cucumber, purple onion, croutons, cheese, and alfalfa sprouts

Chicken Salad - Chicken salad served on a bed of mixed greens with a sliced tomato

Tuna Salad - Tuna salad served on mixed greens with a sliced tomato

Sandwiches

Ham and Cheese - Lean sliced buffet ham, American cheese, leaf lettuce, sliced tomato, and purple onion

Turkey and Cheese - Sliced turkey breast, Swiss cheese, leaf lettuce, sliced tomato, and purple onion

Roast Beef and Cheese - Roast beef, American cheese, leaf lettuce, sliced tomato, and purple onion

French Dip - Hot roast beef with a side of au jus

Hot Pastrami - Hot pastrami, leaf lettuce, sliced tomato, purple onion, and mustard

Chicken Salad - Chicken salad, leaf lettuce, sliced tomato, and purple onion

Tuna Salad - Tuna salad, leaf lettuce, sliced tomato, and purple onion

The Garden Sandwich - Avocado, sliced tomato, mushrooms, leaf lettuce, alfalfa sprouts, purple onion, and cream cheese

Pimento Cheese Sandwich - Pimento cheese served on choice of bread

Ham, Turkey, Roast Beef and Cheese - Served with American cheese, leaf lettuce, sliced tomato, and purple onion

Submarine - Ham, turkey, pastrami, and American cheese served with leaf lettuce, sliced tomato, and purple onion

Hughes Springs

 Antiques America

117 E. First Street
903-639-2466

"He makes the steaks and she bakes the cakes" at the Antiques America Tearoom and Grill. Run by the mother and son team of Elaine and Clint Julian, Antiques America originally served as Hughes Springs' donut shop until the former owner started California dreaming. Elaine bought the business and expanded it to include gourmet pies and decorator cakes. Eventually the donuts moved to California too, and Elaine converted the store into an antique mall and a tearoom with an impressive dessert list.

Clint later added the grill at the back of the store to cater to the avid sports population pining for a post-game T-bone. He designed the room in the same red, white, and blue Americana theme as the tearoom, but with a cobalt blue counter and barstools instead of crazy quilt tablecloths and old photographs.

The specialty of the tearoom is the broccoli cheese soup, sold by the gallon to queso connoisseurs from Louisiana and on demand from locals. Clint's special edition chili, the masterpiece of the grill, has yet to be entered into the town's annual horseshoe tournament and chili cookoff. Perhaps he doesn't wish to take unfair advantage of the other competitors.

If you are visiting from out of town, aim for a Saturday. Hughes Springs takes its local sports very seriously. Although Antiques America remains open, many of the former spa town's businesses hang "gone to the game" signs on their doors. If you plan it right, you can nosh in bliss on your peppermint cake with the old-fashioned seven-minute icing while the rest of the population spurs its team on to greatness at the stadium.

House Tea: Orange Pekoe (The folks in Hughes Springs like their tea straight up.)

Hours: (Store and tearoom) Mon.-Sat. 9-5; (Grill) Mon.-Sat. 11-3

Location: On main street through town

Extended Services: Wedding and Baby Showers, Rehearsal Dinners, Bakery, Candy, Grill

Menu

Salads

Garden Salad   Chef Salad
Chicken Salad   Tuna Salad

Sandwiches

BLT   Tuna Salad
Chicken Salad   Ham
Turkey   Club Sandwich

 ## Honeysuckle Rose

115 N. Ward Street
903-639-1808

Everybody sing, "Tea for two and two for tea." If you are unsure of the lyrics, make sure you sit at the table with the correct sheet music, otherwise you might find "I Left My Heart in San Francisco" or "Send Me the Pillow You Dream On." The Honeysuckle Rose tearoom reflects owner Carol Sikule's love of music. Old scores lay at each setting under the glass. Vintage saxophones, collected from Carol's husband's instrument repair business, dot the walls. In deference to the name of the tearoom, which is also a song, the handful of tables in the intimate tearoom are draped with rose painted tablecloths. The dishes have a rose pattern, and even the menus are printed on glossy red rose cards.

The gift room next door stocks something for everyone. Painted shirts, hand embroidered towels, and shelves made by Carol with distressed barn wood share the floor space with bird feeders and floor-to-ceiling cabinets filled with antique fishing reels. A ceramic lighthouse makes foghorn noises as you walk by.

Carol and Jim Sikule recently moved to Hughes Springs to convert the former funeral home into a tearoom and gift shop. The restored second floor will soon be the new home of the Sikules, who decided to leave the country life and move in with the two resident benevolent ghosts.

House Tea: Orange Pekoe with Grenadine

Hours: Tues.-Sat. 10-3

Location: One block off the main street

Extended Services: Wedding and Baby Showers, Rehearsal Dinners

Kilgore

 ## Miss B's Bridal and Tearoom

104 North Kilgore Street
903-983-1230

From a distance they resemble a collection of bizarre radio towers. Each topped with the Lone Star in lights, these oil derricks are the legacy of Kilgore, home of the Rangerettes. In its heyday, "the richest little acre in the world" had over two thousand derricks drilling for oil as fast as folks could construct them. So many fortunes were made here, that when the Lou de la Creme Number One hit its famous gusher around the turn of the century, its owner told the drillers they would have to wait for her. She was late for church.

At one time over twenty-five derricks elbowed each other on the corner where the Western Union turned dress shop turned Miss B's Tearoom now resides. When Barbara Dougherty was a girl, she couldn't afford any of the dresses they sold at the shop on the driller's pay of her father. Now she sells wedding gowns and tea there.

The front of the store is devoted to Barbara's business of twenty-two years, bridal one-stop shopping. The back of the store houses the tearoom with the white picket fence and the peppermint striped wallpaper. As one customer said, "It looks just like home. Even the wallpaper is the same at my house."

Barbara runs both shops but doesn't give herself top billing. On her menu is written:

Proprietor: God

Laborer: Barbara Dougherty

She says that the owner is an exacting boss, but the benefits are fabulous.

House Tea: Raspberry, Blackberry, and Apple Spice

Hours: (Store) Mon.-Fri. 10-4, Sat. 9-5; (Lunch) Mon.-Sat. 11-2, 6-9 P.M.

Location: Downtown

Extended Services: Wedding and Baby Showers, Rehearsal Dinners, Receptions, Catering, Children's Dress-Up, Bridal Shop

Marshall

 The Friend Home

801 W. Houston
903-934-9227

"Blessed is he who has learned to laugh at himself, for he shall never cease to be entertained." This motto and a variety of others adorn the ceiling of the Friend Home Bed and Breakfast and Tearoom. About eight blocks from downtown Marshall, this lavish turn-of-the-century gingerbread house looks like it hasn't aged a day.

Shepherds frolic on the Victorian reproduction wallpaper that wraps each room. The ornate fireplaces with the carved mantels compliment the tall ceilings and dark hued swags draping the twelve-foot windows. The most striking feature of the house, the woodwork, is seen in intricately carved door moldings, inset cabinets of mahogany, aristocratic furniture, and a spidery lattice that fills the entryway. The doors all have transoms to let the air in or for the mother-in-law to eavesdrop, depending on which story you hear.

The tea itself is always served in French presses as the owner, Penny Ryan, custom blends all of the flavors. Currently, Penny is also creating a tearoom in St. Augustine, Florida, in a house very similar to this one. And you thought you had a long commute.

House Tea: Angel Falls Mist, Ginger Peach, and Berry Berry

Hours: (Continental Breakfast) Tues.-Sat. 7-9:30; (Mid-Morning Tea) Tues.-Sat. 9:30-11; (Lunch) Tues.-Sat. 11-2; (Tea) Tues.-Sat. 2-5; (Dinner) Tues.-Sat. 5-8 P.M.

Location: Off Highway 80W, eight blocks from downtown

Extended Services: Wedding and Baby Showers, Rehearsal Dinners, Receptions, Bed and Breakfast, Facials and Manicures, Custom Blended Tea and Perfume

 ## Three Friends

508 E. Grand Avenue
903-938-1788

A few blocks from downtown Marshall sits a pair of houses that a devoted father built for his daughters in the 1880s. He made one small and ornate because the daughter had no children. The other he made bigger and simpler so the grandchildren would-n't wreck it. The larger of the two buildings is now home to the Winding Wisteria gift shop and the Three Friends Tearoom.

Folks traveling to Mar-shall's popular Wonderland of Lights or Jefferson's Mardi Gras stop by Three Friends for a good meal, to revisit the rooms in which they might have once lived when Winding Wisteria was

a boardinghouse, and to catch a glimpse of the resident ghost. No one knows who the lady is who stands in the window overlooking the yard, but several people have waved at her only to find that there was no one upstairs.

The multiple rooms, each in shades of blue, peach, or lilac, often are filled with simultaneous parties. Children prefer to dine from their Mary Engelbreit dishes in the room upstairs with the white picket fence and floral wallpaper.

At Winding Wisteria, Pam Wright and Charlotte Courtney still offer their original custom candle business. Guests who visit the new dinner buffet receive a free votive candle with the scent of the week, many of which are designed to make you suitably hungry. How's that for good marketing?

House Tea: Raspberry Rhapsody

Hours: Mon.-Sat. 10-9

Location: Behind St. Joseph Catholic Church

Extended Services: Wedding and Baby Showers, Rehearsal Dinners, Receptions, Children's Dress-Up

Mineola

 ## Miss Scarlett's

408 S. Pacific
903-569-5316

"As God is my witness, I'll never be hungry again!" And you won't be if you frequent Miss Scarlett's, the Victorian tearoom in the heart of the rail-road town of Mineola. Inside the converted furniture store, the faux ante-bellum porch leads you into the salon. Period lamps cast a romantic glow upon the mauve floral walls, dark green carpeting, and Victorian knickknacks. The vintage memorabilia are not only *not* for sale, but in fact are glued to the shelves. The owner's husband says he doesn't want to have to redecorate.

The tearoom, the adjoining dress shop, and Scarlett's garden, the muraled terrace room reserved for private parties, are run by the West clan. Started by the mother and daughter, now mother, Barbara, and son, Scott, do all the cooking. The patriarch lends a hand when he gets a few minutes to rub together from the renowned Mineola stage theater he

administers. Even the items on the menu reflect the names of the family members and grandchildren.

Next time you want to take in lunch and a matinee, make the short hop east of Dallas to Mineola. The local stage repertoire rotates, so if musicals make you wince, check out the drama the following week. After all, tomorrow is another day.

House Tea: Vanilla, Raspberry, and Peach Praline

Hours: Tues.-Sat. 11-2

Location: Across the railroad tracks

Extended Services: Wedding and Baby Showers, Rehearsal Dinners

Menu

Salads

Master Leo's Chef Salad   Master J's Dinner Salad
Miss Sara's Grilled Chicken Salad

Sandwiches

The Charleston - Chicken salad on a croissant

The Plantation - Club sandwich with ham, turkey, and bacon

Miss Alexandra - Bacon with avocado on a croissant

Miss Alayna - Smoked turkey on a croissant

Miss Allison - Chicken breast with avocado on a croissant

Entrees

Master Lee - Baked potato with butter and sour cream

Master Thomas - Baked potato with butter, sour cream, green onions, bacon, and cheese

Master Brad - Baked potato with butter, sour cream, ham, and cheese

Master Scott - Baked potato with turkey, cheese, butter, and sour cream

Miss Barbara's Quiche

Mount Pleasant

Our Special Touch

112 W. 2nd
(Inside Chatti Cathie's Gallery)
903-572-0779

Where once strains of Tommy Dorsey and the big band sound floated off the brick walls of downtown, now the rhythmic pounding of Luchese heels echo in synchronization to the whiny violins of country line dance music. For twenty-five years, the Orange Blossom Special Ballroom has beckoned happy feet to the Main Street city of Mount Pleasant. The genre has changed with the times, but the desire to dance the night away has evidently not dissipated over the years. If you dance all night and all morning, you might have burned enough calories to make friends with the banana split cheesecake at Our Special Touch Tearoom.

Stashed in the back of Chatti Cathie's Frame Shop, Special Touch gives the town something to dance about. The basic menu enjoys chalkboard additions, like apple dumplings and Mandarin orange salad. The scattered tables on the main floor and up the ramp to the party rooms wear country elegant cloths in a dark green floral that looks at home among the high ceilings and dated brick walls. If you are an architecture fan, take a look at the brick arch behind the ramp. The original floor of the mercantile lies six feet below the ramp, and two feet of arch still marks where cargo was unloaded onto carts. Aren't old buildings great!

House Tea: Friendship Tea

Hours: (Store) Mon.-Sat. 10-5; (Lunch) Mon.-Sat. 11-2

Location: Downtown

Extended Services: Wedding and Baby Showers, Rehearsal Dinners

Menu

Salads

Grilled Chicken Salad   Chef Salad

Sandwiches

Roast Beef   Club Sandwich
Reuben   Deluxe Sandwich
Grilled Chicken   Chicken Salad
Ham and Cheese   Turkey Sandwich

"Oolong" means "black dragon" in Chinese.

Ore City

 Cherubs

15080 State Highway 155 North
903-968-2180

All night, all day, angels are watching over you at Cherubs. Just north of Gilmer along one of the loveliest stretches of roads in Texas, the little pink house sits next to its own pond surrounded by the piney woods. As you walk past the massive azalea shrubs and through the etched front doors, you can see why *Southern Living Magazine* wrote two articles about this tearoom. The atrium is filled in summer with fountains, angel sculptures, and a weeping willow. In winter, customers can buy ethereal ornaments off the self-snowing tree. On the vaulted ceiling, cherubs flit between the clouds in an azure sky.

The ceiling in the tearoom is painted with angels in the likeness of the owner's grandchildren. On the tables, the dishes are Fitz and Floyd Angel pattern, and even the salt and pepper shakers follow the heavenly theme. It is the food, however, that draws people even from Dallas. Along with a secret recipe chicken salad and a reuben that makes New Yorkers sob with reminiscence, Cherubs whips up specialties from the owner's eighteen-year background in catering. Rock Cornish hens with rice pilaf and homemade bread constitutes one day's special. If you are not a tea fan, you can get alternatives from a vintage Italian cappuccino maker.

This year when you hit the Wildflower Trail, drop the convertible top and zoom along the rural back roads to Cherubs. You can work up an appetite singing, "Oh, What a Beautiful Morning" at the top of your lungs. The cows won't care. They've seen weirder.

House Tea: Mint Julep, Raspberry, or Mango

Hours: Tues.-Sat. 11-3

Location: ½ mile southwest of U.S. 259

Extended Services: Wedding and Baby Showers, Rehearsal Dinners, Catering

Quitman

 ## Courtyard Café

101 Lipscombe Street
903-763-0239

Gentlemen, start your outboards, the bass tournament has begun. Every year happy anglers migrate to Quitman to try their luck at the Lake Fork

Largemouth Bass competition. The 27,700-acre reservoir created by damming the Sabine River has produced thirty-four of the top fifty largest bass ever caught in Texas. The champion, Bubba, weighed in at 18.18 pounds and could probably feed a small nation for a year.

If you prefer chicken salad over sushimi, the Courtyard Café stands ready to pamper fishing widows, festival-goers, and legal eagles from the courthouse across the street. Designed in sage and mauve with a cascading waterfall in the corner and bowls of flowers on the tables, the café lends tranquillity to the busy festival goings-on. Just follow the white picket fence.

If you can't make it for the fishing tourney, try the Dogwood Festival held in honor of the thousands of native dogwood trees blooming in Quitman's surrounding undeveloped acreage. If you have time, stay for the Queen's Tea and the Little Miss Dogwood Tea and coronation. Despite the title of the latter, the child who is crowned is not necessarily the one who looks most like a dogwood.

Incidentally, Quitman was also the home of James Hogg, Texas's first native governor. Contrary to popular belief, he didn't name his daughter Ima out of a twisted sense of humor. He thoughtlessly named his angelic baby after a character in his beloved brother's Civil War epic, *The Fate of Marvin*. Ima's grandfather is said to have nearly killed his horse riding to prevent his son from making such a lamentable choice in names. But it was too late; she'd already been christened.

House Tea: Strawberry Kiwi, Peach, and Black Cherry

Hours: Mon.-Fri. 11-2

Location: On the square

Extended Services: Wedding and Baby Showers, Rehearsal Dinners, Receptions, Children's Dress-Up

> "Matrons, who toss the cup, and see
> The grounds of fate in grounds of
> tea..."
>   – Alexander Pope

Tyler

 ## Tyler Square Tearoom

117 S. Broadway
903-535-9994

The city of Tyler takes its tea drinking so seriously that it even named a rose after it. Haven't you ever heard of Tyler Tea roses? Every year from far and near tourons pop their Claritin and flock to this genteel town to inhale deeply, watch parades, and see what a little sandy loam, a lot of hard work, and a healthy heap of cow manure can produce. The city fairly bursts with roses of every kind; long stemmed, rambling, hedge, and fairy wrap the old plantation homes in an aroma so intoxicating, your sinuses will be smiling for days.

When your eyes, nose, and feet have gone into sudden death overtime, visit Tyler Square Tearoom where the good folk will "fix you some tea and treat you like an East Texan should." The tearoom sprawls across the balcony of a 1940s Sears and Roebuck-turned-antique mall. The overhead lights still have their original pull chains that take employees thirty minutes to turn on. Greeting you on the green and mauve tables are baskets of secret recipe sugar cookies that will surely ruin you for all others.

If you arrive on certain days, you may see the bridge club or the mahjong group playing at their favorite tables. When Sandy Duncan comes home to Tyler, she pops in for the Banana Split Salad, which contains bananas and three scoops of chicken, tuna, or potato salad in a banana boat with a cherry. On your way out, if you pull the rug back on the street entrance to the building, you'll see the Sears name still written in tile at the door.

House Tea: Raspberry

Hours: (Store) Mon.-Sat. 10-5:30, Sun. 11-5; (Lunch) Mon.-Fri. 11-2 (open on Saturdays during the Azalea and Rose festivals)

Location: Downtown

Extended Services: Wedding and Baby Showers, Rehearsal Dinners, Receptions, Private Parties

---

Tea shrubs take five years to develop but produce for fifty years.

Two-water teas can be steeped twice with equal flavor.

More Assam and African teas are produced than Darjeeling or Ceylon because the terrain is flatter.

Southeast

Tastes Great, Less Filling

Add novelty to your friends' humdrum lives, or spice a shower by throwing a tea-tasting party. A great time can be had by all for a few cups of H_2O, a handful of flakes, and a group of people with an ample sense of humor.

In preparation, gather some snackies to cleanse the palate. Chocolate always tops the list for popularity, and you'll never have to worry what to do with the leftovers. Visit your local tea merchant for a variety of tea samples, or order them in advance on the Internet. Dallas and Houston boast quite excellent stores, but if you don't know of one in your area, look in the Yellow Pages under "C" for "coffee." (Go figure.)

When you visit the store, choose two or three types of green tea, a few black, possibly some oolong, and maybe a few miscellaneous, like white tea or a black and green blend. Remember that you only need a couple of teaspoons per pot, so a minimal amount of each will allow you to splurge on some exclusive tastes, like Jasmine buds. The owner of the shop will probably lend you some excellent suggestions if you confess your plans.

Before folks arrive, set out the sugar, honey, and whatnot and start the kettles boiling. Use distilled water if possible for the purest flavor. Make the green teas first before the water comes to a boil. Boiling flattens the flavor of greens. Steep them for only two to three minutes in a clay pot or Brown Betty and strain into your designer teapot. Now is your chance to show off your collection. Mark the bottom of the pot with the name of the tea and pop a cozy over it to keep it warm. Steep the black teas for three to five minutes in boiled water.

To complete the setup, line the pots in groups according to their types so your guests can do some comparison sipping, then clean the watercloset. Your guests will probably have a nodding acquaintance with this room before the evening ends.

When your victims arrive, hand them cue cards of Tea Speak words so they can sound like proper snobs. Here are some official terms, but feel free to invent words of your own.

Burnt	Sweaty	Bright	Bouquet
Soapy	Full Body	Light	Flowery
Cloudy	Fragrant	Dull	Tainted
Brisk	Astringent	Flat	Harsh

Although the official method for testing includes slurping the liquid off a spoon at the back of the palate, swishing it around the mouth while inhaling deeply, and expectorating it into a nearby spittoon, this does tend to wreck the carpets. So, splashing each teacup with just a spot to catch the taste will probably work better. Once everyone has tried a group and discussed the merits of each tea, effusively sowing adjectives along the way, read the name and the trade symbols for that variety. Everyone can nod knowingly and go back to consuming chocolate and gabbing.

SFTGFOP	Special Finest Tippy Golden Flowery Orange Pekoe	pretty darn good
TGFOP	Tippy Golden Flowery Orange Pekoe	not half bad
FOP	Flowery Orange Pekoe	ditto
OP	Orange Pekoe	not really the good stuff
BOP	Broken Orange Pekoe	the daily grind
Dust	What you make for the neighbors who come over to borrow your lawnmower	grocery grade

Other fun activities for the evening can include: Pin the Spout on the Teapot, reading tea leaves, the Price is Right (guessing which kind is the most expensive), or estimating how many calories were consumed *in toto* from all of the chocolate.

Bon appetit.

Beaumont

 ## Two Magnolias

2910 East Tex Freeway
(Inside Ashton House)
409-899-4847

Through the back roads and fields of Beaumont, Babe Zaharias ran, keeping in shape for the basketball games, the swimming matches, the golf games, and the track meets. Although she gained fame by winning seventeen consecutive women's golf tournaments in the 1930s and '40s, and the National Women's Open after cancer surgery in the '50s, Babe also set world records in the 1932 Olympic Games for the eighty-meter hurdles and javelin throw for which she received three gold medals. Besides the baseball, football, tennis, boxing, and swimming events in which she competed, Babe was also named basketball All American three times. In her spare time, she played billiards and knitted.

After visiting the museum and memorial park dedicated to this great athlete, you will be ready to rest from the thirty years of sports events in which you just competed vicariously.

> "Ecstasy is a glass full of tea and a piece of sugar in the mouth."
>
> – Aleksandr Pushkin

The southern plantation-style tearoom of Two Magnolias sits right around the corner.

Started as a permanent site for Storybook Weddings, the bridal event coordination business created by the owners, Two Magnolias fills the second floor of Ashton House with ivy-covered lattices, magnolia-draped Greek columns, and crispy white linens. Quiche remains the specialty of the house, and if you are feeling adventurous, try the excellent crab and jalapeño quiche. It's so light, you won't be weighed down when you leap those hurdles home.

House Tea: Raspberry and Peach

Hours: (Store) Mon.-Sat. 10-4; (Lunch) Mon.-Fri. 11-2

Location: Delaware and East Tex Freeway

Extended Services: Wedding and Baby Showers, Rehearsal Dinners, Catering, Children's Dress-Up, Wedding Coordination

Two's Company

6290 Phelan
409-860-7233

With a boom the famous Spindletop oil gusher of 1901 created the Golden Triangle city of Beaumont. The lumber and rice mills became extinct overnight, and three oil companies were born; the Texas Company now known as Texaco, Humble Oil, later named Exxon, and the one named for the nearby body of water, Gulf Oil Corporation. Although the petro-chemical industry still plays a major role in the port city, the revitalization of downtown now attracts a crowd more interested in the price of a painting than bucks per barrel. A favorite oasis for bargain hunters both native and passing through is Two's Company Tearoom and Bakery.

The green canopy welcomes you off the street and into the cozy café. In the dim light, antique sideboards lean against the beige and green walls, and foliage rustles as you jockey among the mauve linen tables. At lunch the trendy fashion becomes scrubs as the tearoom fills with doctors and staff from the surrounding hospitals. The smell of newly iced wedding cake permeates the air. Two's Company has a thriving side business as a bakery, which stays open after lunch hours for evening cravings. On the street you'll pass shoppers toting bags of their homemade cookies.

If you get the chance, plan your visit during the Neches River Festival held in honor of the noble river that spawned Beaumont. The festival and the South Texas State Fair draw hordes of corny dog connoisseurs toward the coast.

House Tea: Raspberry

Hours: Mon.-Sat. 11-3

Location: Phelan and Dowlen in the Colonnade Shopping Center

Extended Services: Wedding and Baby Showers, Rehearsal Dinners, Receptions, Catering, Bakery

"Tea's proper use is to amuse
the idle and relax the studious
and dilute the full meals of
those who cannot use exercise
and will not use abstinence."

– Samuel Johnson

Bryan

 Clementines

202 S. Bryan
(Inside Old Bryan Marketplace)
979-779-2558

The Aggies would be appalled to learn of the sheer number of "T-sippers" in their hometown. Bryan's best-kept secret, Clementines, attracts many more guests than just the Gig-folk. As you step inside the timberframe entrance of the Old Bryan Marketplace, the eyes are met with a myriad of colors and scenes organized into topical vignettes across the turn-of-the-century hardware store. Restored by owner and passionate garage sale "junker" Kay Conlee, the Marketplace has received much acclaim and numerous awards for design and originality, including a Historical Presentation Award and articles in *Southern Living* and the *Wall Street Journal*. Antiques, handmade furniture, landscape items, boutique clothes, and assorted memorable gifts scatter across the 22,000-square-foot floor separated by authentic Robertson County jail bars.

On the right, the chic New Orleans-style tearoom, called café, caters to enthusiastic crowds. Known primarily for their bread pudding served caramelized by the chef's propane torch, Clementines dishes its shrimp salads and tomato basil soup among the black and white decor.

> Only the tip and top two leaves of the youngest shoots are used for tea.

Bentwood chairs surround glass tables with black napkins, and antique rugs cover the pine floors and nudge the ancient brick walls with corbels. Chandeliers from the Mississippi riverboat *Delta Queen* sparkle overhead. Even if you don't have business at the nearby George Bush Museum or the genealogy library, Clementines is a reason unto itself to visit downtown Bryan.

House Tea: Peach

Hours: (Store) Mon.-Sat. 10-6; (Lunch) Mon.-Sat. 11-3

Location: Downtown

Extended Services: Wedding and Baby Showers, Rehearsal Dinners

Menu

Salads

Caesar Salad - Served with homemade garlic croutons and shaved Parmesan cheese

Angel Hair Pasta and Shrimp Salad - Served with julienne carrots, field greens, and cilantro with sesame soy vinaigrette, raisins, and sesame seeds

Greek Salad with Feta Cheese - Tomato, red onion, feta cheese, and Calamata olives on mixed greens, accompanied by olive oil, lemon, and oregano vinaigrette

Sandwiches

Grilled Chicken with Jack Cheese - Served on herb focaccia bread, topped with bacon, avocado, lettuce, and tomato, accompanied with cilantro mayonnaise

Marketplace Sandwich - Grilled eggplant, zucchini, sautéed mushrooms, roasted red bell peppers, Monterey Jack cheese, lettuce, tomato, and field greens, served on a toasted multigrain bun with pesto mayonnaise

Smoked Turkey and Melted Brie - Served on focaccia bread, topped with lettuce, tomato, and cilantro mayonnaise

Old-Fashioned Chicken Salad - Served with tomato and lettuce on a croissant

Caldwell

 The Mad Hatter

210 S. Echols
409-567-3504

Every Thursday, Jeanie Price swaps her nurse's hat for a mad hat. As a cardiology RN, Jeanie works at a hospital in Bryan the first of the week, then opens the doors of the Mad Hatter Tearoom for the long weekend. Naturally, entrees like the signature curry and raisin chicken salad are made with skim milk and heart healthy ingredients. The items on the menu reflect names from Alice in Wonderland, like Mock Turtle Soup and Cater-pillar Pie, which has a chocolate crust and pistachio ice cream.

Customers often donate the hats that cover the walls of the 1800s two-story and are worn by every member of the staff, including the cook. The silver pine, dark forest green, and ashes of roses coloring compliments the original pressed tin ceiling and gingerbread-trimmed serving window. The faux window Jeanie rendered on the back wall serves as a reminder of the painting studio that she originally intended for the building. Upstairs, the red tin ceilings hang over Lawyer's Landing, the bed and breakfast named in honor of the Tennessee lawyer who first owned the building.

If you plan to stay, Caldwell is a hop, skip, and a jump from aqua parties at nearby Lake Summerville, vintage tasting sessions at Messina Hof Winery, and Czech singalongs at the Kolache festival in September.

House Tea: Peach

Hours: Thurs.-Sat. 8-5 P.M.

Location: Downtown

Extended Services: Wedding and Baby Showers, Rehearsal Dinners, Catering, Children's Dress-Up, Afternoon Tea

Menu

Salads

The Queen's Knave - Traditional Caesar salad, Romaine mix topped with croutons and Parmesan

The Red Queen's Garden Salad - A small dinner salad of crisp greens

Sandwiches

Tweedledee - Ham presented on wheat sourdough bun, lightly dressed with honey mustard, lettuce, tomato, and red onion

The Duchess Delight - Chicken salad served on a croissant

Entrees

Alice's Magic Mushroom Quiche - Combination of mushrooms and Italian seasonings and baked in a homemade crust

Queen of Hearts Quiche - Stuffed with Monterey Jack cheese, Canadian bacon, and green chilies

Cypress

 Idyl Hours Tearoom and Café

12639 Kluge Road
281-370-2626

Nestled among the tranquil pine trees of rural Houston reposes Idyl Hours, a retreat from the city's hustle and bustle. As you walk up the crunchy gravel driveway, the swaying porch swing beckons you to put your feet up. Sit a spell and let your blood pressure drop to medically approved levels, or sidle inside and let the owners welcome you like family. As a retirement present to themselves, Idyl Hours allows Sonny and Nina Riley to do what they love best; cook, talk with folks, paint, and work together.

Evidence of the landlady's favorite pastime covers the walls. The murals and the lovely scrollwork on the tables are all painted by Nina. She uses the entire tearoom as her canvas. The menu also reflects the owners' diversity. The soups are specially created by Sonny, and the pastichio, mousaka, and spinach pie recipes descend directly from Nina's Greek family. The unusual cuisine and the homespun, unfrilly atmosphere assures a large male following.

The specialty woodwork serves as a favorite hobby of the landlord. The rocking elephants, wooden angels, and caned chairs are handmade and sell fast. The front porch usually sports their trademark rocking chair. But if the porch is bare when you visit, someone probably just bought it. You will have to try again in a couple of days. They just can't make the rockers faster than people want them.

House Tea: Red Raspberry and Black Current

Hours: Tues.-Fri. 11-2:30; Tues. 5:30 P.M.-8:30 P.M.

Location: ½ mile off Grant Road

Extended Services: Wedding and Baby Showers, Rehearsal Dinners

Menu

Salads

Chicken Jicama Salad - Crunchy sliced jicama with chunks of chicken breast tossed with a cilantro, honey, and garlic dressing

Greek Salad - Tomato, cucumber, bell pepper, red onion, olives, and feta cheese

Basil Parmesan Chicken Salad   Caesar Salad

Walnut Tortellini with Artichoke Hearts

Sandwiches

Veggie Sandwich - Layered with lettuce, cucumber, tomato, red onions, Swiss cheese, sprouts, and homemade herb mayonnaise

Southwest BLT - Lettuce, tomato, Canadian bacon, and a homemade garlic jalapeño mayonnaise

Entrees

Mushroom Quiche - Sautéed mushroom and herb quiche topped with a yogurt cucumber sauce

Traditional Greek Foods - Spinach pie, pastichio, mousaka, meatballs and brown rice with Greek baked beans, chicken strudel, baked beef with pasta, stuffed bell pepper with potatoes and carrots

Friendswood

The Charleston Tearoom

154 S. Friendswood Drive
281-992-8327

Outside Houston lies the city of Friendswood, named for the Society of Friends church formed by the Quaker founding fathers. Their "everyone is of the light" philosophy is reflected in the family-oriented community as well as the businesses. The people of Friendswood welcome visitors with a refreshing respect of equals often lacking in the big cities. Possibly it is for this reason that the Charleston Tearoom remains perpetually busy during their hours of operation with local folks, church groups, and an enormous number of Houston escapees.

Russians drink their Lapsang Souchong tea extra strong, extra hot, and with a sugar cube between the front teeth.

Across the large floral carpet, the patient waitstaff bustle between the dusty rose and army green tables, brushing the tieback bows on the chairs. Laughter and the hum of voices mingle over the plates of Cheddar Pasta Toss and Apricot tea. Charleston's specialty is baked potato soup, but don't miss the lemon meringue pie or the Hummingbird cake, made with bananas, coconut, and pineapple. Everyone who orders a salad receives the Charleston Delight, a frozen concoction of Cool Whip, pineapple, strawberries, and cream cheese. A cross between dessert and a frozen fruit cocktail, customers buy it by the container for late night refrigerator raids. Their Apricot or Raspberry teas are offered every day, but for a novelty, try the Gourmet Strawberry Lemonade. Great to drink, tough to replicate.

House Tea: Apricot and Raspberry

Hours: Mon.-Sat. 11-2

Location: FM 2351 and Highway 518

Extended Services: Wedding and Baby Showers, Rehearsal Dinners, Catering

Menu

Salads

Spinach Salad - Spinach greens topped with sliced mushrooms, chopped eggs, red onions, and crumbled bacon

The Charleston Salad - Crisp greens topped with roast beef, breast of turkey, cheddar cheese, chopped eggs, purple cabbage, carrots, and tomato

Chunky Chicken Salad - Chunks of chicken, celery, apple, and nuts served on a bed of salad greens

Tuna Salad - Chunks of white meat tuna, egg, celery, pickle relish in a creamy mayonnaise served on a bed of salad greens

Cheddar Pasta Toss - Tri-colored rotini, red onion, and black olives blended with light homemade dressing and garnished with shredded cheddar.

Sandwiches

The Charleston Club - Slices of roasted beef, turkey, and bacon with Swiss cheese, lettuce, and tomato

Roasted Turkey - Slices of roasted turkey breast with dressing of hard-boiled eggs, chopped spinach, and gourmet mayonnaise

Chicken Salad Sandwich - A combination of diced chicken, celery, apples, and pecans served on a croissant

Tuna Salad Sandwich - White meat tuna, eggs, celery, and pickle relish

Primo Pimento - Pimento cheese with slices of bacon, slightly melted and served open-faced

French Dip - Tender pieces of roast beef au jus served open-faced with Swiss cheese on a French roll

"Infusing" a tea means a short soak. "Steeping" means a long soak.

Galveston

The Tremont Hotel

2300 Ships Mechanic Row
409-763-0300

When you feel your gills quivering, Galveston beckons you to the sea. The pounding surf and squawk of gulls sound the same now as they did when Cabeza de Vaca shipwrecked here over 400 years ago. For well over a century, this stomping ground of pirate Jean Laffite thrived as a major shipping port with a population greater than Dallas until very recently. Galveston enjoyed the status as the primary playground of the idle rich until the great hurricane of 1900 decimated the city. As a result, a seventeen-foot-high seawall was erected to protect the town. One of the few buildings to survive that hurricane and another fifteen years later was the Tremont.

The original owners eventually abandoned the building after the Strand fire of 1879. Almost 100 years later Cynthia and George Mitchell converted it into the stately hotel that exists today.

The Tremont offers formal Afternoon Tea in the lovely Victorian lobby. You can sink into overstuffed chairs, listen to the live piano music, and partake of the cucumber sandwiches. When you get your second wind, there is still time to do some serious financial damage in the intriguing shops of the Strand.

Peppermint and Chamomile teas are naturally decaffeinated.

Lightly brewed Oolong contains less caffeine than Black, but Green has less than either.

Green tea remains an excellent source of vitamin C. In black tea the vitamin is destroyed during the fermentation process.

House Tea: English Breakfast

Hours: Hotel open 24 hours, (Tea) Mon.-Sun. 3-5

Location: One block behind the Strand at 23rd Street

Extended Services: Afternoon Tea

Highlands

 ## The Teapot Depot

112 Denny Street
281-426-3670

Long ago, the InterUrban train chugged its way through the backwoods of
Northshore, Highlands, Baytown, and Wallisville, bringing supplies and
commercial traffic from nearby Houston. In Highlands, it would stop at the
Old Elena Train Station and deposit the daily commuters. The station
doesn't exist anymore except in memories and in a mural painted on the
back wall of the Teapot Depot. Located across the railroad tracks from
where the train station once stood, the tearoom is a celebration of the rails
and an all-around great place to get together.

Outside, the railroad crossing sign points you through the white picket
fence to the front yard. In the spring, yellow Jasmine burst through the
fence slats and wind up the lamp posts. In summer, crepe myrtles flank the
walkway, dropping hot pink blossoms at your feet as you ascend the stairs.
The garden is so alive with its trees and windsocks that it is tempting to

take tea at the bistro tables on the verandah. If you do, you won't get a chance to check out the faux table linens inside.

Step over the mural of the teapot painted on the front stoop. Once inside choose from three dining rooms. Most men prefer the Train Room in the back. The mural of the InterUrban and station was painted by Sue Norris, who also did all the artwork in their cookbook. If you pick the right day, you may run into Lee Dunn, the first conductor of the InterUrban, who dines in this room for old times' sake when visiting his daughter.

If you eat in one of the other rooms, you will be seated at the tables made by the owner's husband. From a distance they appear to be simple square tables with cloths drapes over them. A closer inspection reveals that they are all carved out of wood and painted to look that way.

The sandwiches are named after train occupations, such as the Brakeman's Plate and the Ticket Agent's Preference, which is apparently tuna salad. If you want something different, try the Flower Pot Pie. It is literally baked in a flower pot.

As you leave the Depot, a little sign among the azaleas reads, "My favorite recipe is eating out." The owners are obviously kindred spirits.

House Tea: Hot Spiced Tea

Hours: Tues.-Fri. 10:30-2, Sat. 11-3

Location: Across from the railroad tracks just outside of Houston

Extended Services: Wedding and Baby Showers, Rehearsal Dinners, Receptions, Catering, Delivery

Menu

Salads

Southwest Chicken Salad - Grilled chicken breast on mixed lettuce with cheese, black olives, tomato, and avocado with light Italian dressing

Chef Salad - A green salad with ham, turkey, American cheese, Swiss cheese, boiled eggs, and a sweet cherry pepper

Pasta Salad - Marinated rotini pasta, black olives, broccoli, tomato, and pimento cheese

Small Green Salad - Mixed lettuce with shredded carrots and purple cabbage, tomato, and cucumber slices

Mandarin Orange Salad - Mandarin orange slices and slivered almonds on mixed lettuce with a poppy seed dressing

Sandwiches

Turkey Reuben - Fat-free turkey and mozzarella cheese, sauerkraut, mustard, and spices on pumpernickel

Hobo Veggie Sandwich - Cream cheese, black olives, cucumbers, tomato, mushrooms, and sprouts on poppy seed bread

Texas Club - Ham, turkey, American cheese, Swiss cheese, lettuce, and tomato

Casey Jones - Chicken salad

Flagman's Preference - Pimento cheese

Trainmaster's #1 - Ham and American cheese

Trainmaster's #2 - Smoked turkey and Swiss cheese

Ticket Agent's Preference - Tuna salad

Engineer's Special - Roast beef and American cheese

Caboose - Peanut butter and jelly

Entrees

Flower Pot Pie - Chicken and vegetables in a creamy sauce baked in custom clay pot with pastry crust

Houston

 Ashland House

7611 Westview Drive
713-682-5664

Pardon me, but isn't that a tree growing in your living room? Actually, there are two oak trees growing through the roof of this garden center turned tearoom. Ashland was once located in a powder blue Victorian house in the Heights, the image of which is lovingly rendered on the back wall of one of the party rooms. When they moved to their new location in this woody suburban area, Ashland inherited the natural beauty already present.

More of a restaurant than a tearoom, Ashland House serves formal teas and special functions as well as their standard menu in the cleverly designed restaurant. The Garden Room with the oak trees is bright and sunny with skylights in the vaulted roof. Festoons of grapevine and wisteria hang from the ceiling beams, and wooden birdhouses nestle into available niches. The secluded Library Room, named after the wallpaper that resembles antique bookshelves, is small and intimate. Oddly enough, people dining in this room tend to speak in hushed whispers.

The party rooms in the back house long tables for very large groups. For showers, tulle bows are tied around bistro chairs. The tables are elegant in white linens and china, Victorian napkin rings, and valentine red napkins. Crystal knife rests and salt cellars sit at each place setting daring the visitor to guess what they are used for. Ashland House hosts multitudes of showers and special occasions, including a reading incentive program for area schools. If the student reads the prerequisite amount, they get a formal tea in their honor. Drinking it in the Library Room is optional.

House Tea: Apricot

Hours: (Brunch) by reservation only Mon.-Sat. 9:30-11:30; (Lunch) Mon.-Sat. 11-3; (Tea) Mon.-Sat. 2-4

Location: Off Wirt/Antoin

Extended Services: Wedding and Baby Showers, Rehearsal Dinners, Receptions

 Gepetto's Treasures

2419 Robinhood
713-529-2203

Does your Wakeen have the whooping cough, your Madame Alexander the mumps? Send them to Gepetto's Treasures Doll Hospital and tearoom where they'll give them instant resuscitation no matter what HMO plan you have. In the converted residential house of Houston's suburbs, multiple rooms of healthy new artist collectible dolls greet your ailing porcelain puppet with great sympathy, but the humans do the surgery.

To celebrate your friend's complete recovery, invite her to a party in the Tea House. Through the Blue Door, the miniature white furniture and tiny teacups await the arrival of the guests. Play Pin the Spout on the Teapot, then wander into the lush grassy yard for a pony ride around the Victorian dollhouse and floppy-eared bunny cages. Listen to the storyteller, create your own perfume, decorate a hat for your little side-kick, or play a game of croquet against the wicked Queen of Hearts. Be careful, she cheats.

Although Gepetto's caters primarily to children, fantasy theme parties are available for adults. Invite your friends, inanimate or otherwise, and your favorite teddy to celebrate that upcoming wedding or new arrival. Gepetto's throws equal opportunity soirées.

House Tea: Lemonade

Hours: Tues.-Sat. 9:30-5

Location: Behind Kirby Shopping Center

Extended Services: Wedding and Baby Showers, Children's Dress-Up

 Laura's Tearoom and TLC Gallery

2339 Bay Area Boulevard
281-480-1600

"Houston, we have a problem. We're out of Peppermint Chocolate Chip Bread and are scratching the mission. Over."

"This is Houston. Do not abort. We are placing the order at Laura's now and will send it up in the shuttle. Over."

"Roger that, Houston. Over."

Within rock throwing distance of Nassau Space Center, Laura's Tearoom and TLC Gallery feeds the bevy of hungry architects, engineers, and astronauts that blast by. Although Manager Mark Simotas whips up delightful Saturday breakfasts, featuring apricot French toast and eggs Benedict, the tearoom receives its well-deserved reputation from its Afternoon Teas, stylish luncheons, and artistic party trays.

Live flute and oboe sonatas highlight the three-course Afternoon Teas while patrons snack on smoked turkey with cranberry finger sandwiches and lemon curd tarts. Lunch can be served in either the darkly elegant hunter green room with the mahogany furniture and Thomas Kinkade paintings, or in the congenial peppermint-striped room with the white chairs and Sandra Kuck mother-daughter paintings. Or, if you are late for a lift-off, you can grab a brown bag lunch of gourmet goodies. The diverse and generous party trays keep Laura's hopping with corporate orders and catered function traffic. Choose among cream cheese molds with jalapeño sweet hot glaze, finger sandwiches, baby quiches, and junior quesadillas, or go for the fruit with chocolate fondue or Viennese dessert adventure. If you plan on visiting a space station soon, you may want to pick up a shish kebob platter for your tovarishch.

The TLC Gallery part of Laura's consists of fine art and high-end interior design pieces in the rooms adjoining the tearoom. Highland Hills furniture, Swarovski crystal, and Christopher Radko whatnots find a temporary home here along with works by Michael Geary, Thomas Kinkade, and a host of other talented artisans. There's even a pampered baby department for any junior astronauts on their way, but no one will mind if you buy a Gund bunny for yourself.

House Tea: Peach

Hours: (Store) Mon.-Sat. 10-6; (Breakfast) Sat. 8:30-10:30; (Lunch) Mon.-Sat. 11-2:30

Location: By Space Center Boulevard, in the bay area

Extended Services: Wedding and Baby Showers, Rehearsal Dinners, Receptions, Catering, Party Trays

Menu

Salads

Taco Salad   Festive Pasta Salad
Spinach Salad   Garden Salad

Sandwiches

Ham and Cheese on Croissant   Mesquite Smoked Turkey
Tuna Salad on Wheatberry   Chicken Salad on Wheatberry
Garden Vegetable   Cucumber Sandwich
Spinach and Feta Cheese Croissant

Entrees

Monday = Chicken Divan   Thursday = Chicken Parmesan
Tuesday = Layered Enchilada Torte   Friday = King Ranch Chicken
Wednesday = Garden Lasagna   Saturday = Chef's Choice
Quiche   Baked Potato

 Rose Garden Tearoom and Gifts

10750 Grant Road
281-469-2603

A man waltzed into the Rose Garden the other day and asked if they had seen his wife as he was supposed to meet her there for lunch. After five minutes, the woman didn't show and the gentleman told them that while he was waiting, he'd order a chicken salad sandwich. When he finished his lunch and dessert, he shrugged and left. The owner discovered several days later from the man's wife that she did not have a lunch date with him that day; he just wanted some of the Rose Garden's terrific chicken salad.

You really don't have to go to such an extreme to dine at this charming tearoom. Centrally located on Grant Street, Houston's quasi-autobahn since the construction ended, the Rose Garden resides minutes from downtown. Inside, a white lattice wraps the room in a gazebo of mahogany chairs, creamy linens, and sunshine. The ivy-covered trellises separate the satellite rooms of matching greens, creams, pastels, and florals. The Children's room with its tiny white wicker tables and chairs displays pink ballet slippers, dolls, and other ornaments on an upside-down Christmas tree. Owner Jeanie Romero says that it keeps little fingers from deflocking the tree, but it looks so avant-garde, she may have started a new trend.

Just call it an Umbrella Tree. A fireplace adorns the Victorian Room. Mahogany buffets and fern stands guard the cream and burgundy tables adorned with rose-encircled votives. Outside the gazebo, stepping stones lead you through the garden section past wind chimes, a bassinet announcing the baby gift section, and tiny trees with cat or teapot ornaments perched among the crystal, lamps, and animal sculptures.

The relaxed atmosphere of the Rose Garden invites you to sit a spell and savor the "sweetness of friendship," as the Margaret Furlong angel says. Cup in hand, the angel sits at the entrance of the tearoom waiting for someone to pour.

House Tea: Raspberry or Peach

Hours: (Store) Mon.-Fri. 10-6, Sat. 10-5; (Lunch) Mon.-Sat. 11-2 (Tea and Sweets) Mon.-Sat. 3-5

Location: Grant and Jones

Extended Services: Wedding and Baby Showers, Rehearsal Dinners, Catering, Children's Dress-Up, Afternoon Tea, Weddings

Menu

Salads

Grilled Chicken Caesar   Pasta Salad

Sandwiches

Chicken Salad   Shrimp Salad
Ham   Turkey
Roast Beef

Entrees

Quiche du Jour   Crêpe du Jour
Chicken Mushroom Crêpe

"Research shows that regular consumption of tea has been linked to lower risk of both heart disease and cancer."

-- Prevention Magazine, May 1996

Something Different Tearoom

5050 FM 1960 West #130
281-397-9635

Margaret Gorneau said for years that nothing short of a burning bush would get her to move from her beloved Fredericksburg. When her daughter expressed an interest in opening a family-run tearoom, Margaret decided that Houston might qualify as a smoldering shrub. With the combination of great management and her daughter's "God given recipes," Something Different has thrived behind the painted garden rocker on the storefront window.

The tearoom has a charming collection of mismatched tables and chairs, including a large round yellow table, which is known as the "family table." When the peak hours of lunch are over, special guests are invited to dine with the family here. Invitations are coveted and vary daily. Bridge clubs meet weekly at the larger tables, and the party room in back serves as a business meeting room.

The eclectic menu is the brainchild of daughter Rhonda and includes the signature pieces of key lime pie, cornbread from scratch, and an outrageous tortilla soup, which caused one pleased customer to exclaim, "I didn't know there were Mexican food tearooms!"

Viva la difference!

House Tea: Cinnamon Plum, Ginger Peach, Mango, or Blackberry Sage

Hours: (Store) Mon.-Sat. 10-4, (Lunch) Mon.-Sat. 11-3, (Tea) Mon., Wed., Fri. 3-5

Location: Off Champion Forest Road

Extended Services: Wedding and Baby Showers, Rehearsal Dinners, Receptions, Catering, Afternoon Tea, Whole Desserts for Sale

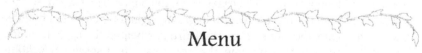

Menu

Salads

Oriental Chicken Salad - Lettuce, cubed chicken, toasted almonds, sesame seeds, green onion, and rice noodles with special dressing

Green Salad - Tossed greens, carrots, celery, cucumber, red cabbage, mushrooms, sprouts, tomato, and homemade croutons

Waldorf Chicken Salad - Chunk white chicken, apple, red grapes, walnuts, and celery with special dressing on a bed of greens

Spring Salad - Mixed greens, candied walnuts, bacon, Parmesan cheese, topped with a balsamic maple vinaigrette

Caesar Salad

Sandwiches

Egg Salad - Hard-boiled egg, onion, dill, sweet relish curry, and herb mayonnaise

Herb Chicken Salad - Chicken breast cubed with green onion, celery, capers, and herb mayonnaise

Jalapeño Pimento Cheese - Mixture of cheeses, pimento, and jalapeños

Boars Head Cracked Pepper Turkey Breast - Served with Monterey Jack cheese, jalapeño mayonnaise, lettuce, and tomato

Boars Head Honey Ham - Honey mustard, with Swiss cheese, lettuce, and tomato

Veggie Sandwich - Herb mayonnaise, lettuce, tomato, cucumbers, sprouts, and Swiss cheese

Grilled Chicken Breast - Marinated for 48 hours and served with jalapeño mayonnaise, lettuce, and tomato

🍽 Tea and More By Patty

(English Tea Parlour Teas)

2428 Times Boulevard
713-526-2995
http://www.englisht-parlort.com

For hundreds of years, Russian caravans crossed the continent to sell their teas to the Mongol hordes. The casks were too bulky to be hauled, so they packed the loose tea leaves in cloth bags. At night as the traders huddled around the camp, the smoke from their fire permeated the bags, leaving a smoky flavored tea that became the trademark of Lapsang Souchong. Even though Russian caravans no longer roam the plains as they once did, Asian customers still demand the smoky taste as a stamp of quality. Commercially, the leaves are now pine roasted before they are packed for market.

The Lapsang Souchong, as well as the interesting history surrounding it are available from Tea and More. As the foremost tea merchants in Houston, owners Chuck and Patty Dennison offer the best of the best to tea connoisseurs nationwide and still find time to share fascinating pieces of trivia. Chuck's time is divided between running the supply shop, servicing orders over the Internet, and giving historical lectures to clubs and universities. He still finds time to explain to customers what a three-water tea is, why green leaves are good for the immune system, and how to make a killer batch of sugar cookies with orange spice.

The narrow store abounds with teapots, gifts, epicurean accessories, and huge jars of loose tea. They carry 165 different teas, everything from the common and inexpensive to the exotic and extravagant. English Breakfast is one of the most popular blends, but if you are feeling adventurous, the Champagne Oolong and the Chocolate Mint after-dinner tea is definitely intriguing. Tea and More is one of the very few places where you can get real Jasmine buds. Drop a couple in your boiling water and they will open into flowers and make a tea so mildly sweet, you won't need sugar.

If you get a chance to talk, ask Chuck to show you a tea brick. In the seventeenth century, China used these bars of pressed tea as currency. Each was embossed with the royal seal, and when you needed some cash, you simply broke off a preprinted rectangle, sort of like an Earl Grey Mastercard.

House Tea: English Breakfast

Hours: Mon.-Fri. 9:30-6, Sat. 9-5

Location: In Rice Village

Extended Services: Merchant, Lectures, Internet Ordering, Catalog
Orders, Information to impress your friends and neighbors

Humble

 Tattletells Tearoom

403 1st Street E
281-319-4832

Roses to the right of them,
Lilies to the left of them,
Freesias in front of them,
"Forward, the Tea Brigade!" to Tattletells.

The hottest spot for showers in Humble lies in carnation camouflage
inside the Elegant Flowers florist shop. Step past the wooden chair suspended from the ancient oak and up the stairs of the Roaring Twenties
brick. A profusion of colors and scents await you just inside. Prowl through
the lush green interior past the orchids and exotics and peer through the
palms. Tattletells lies just beyond.

Oleta Dement offers tea in style with a varied menu that won first
place in Humble's Taste of the Town. Check out the chicken salad made
with almonds and honey. Its recipe can be traced back to the 1800s when
Humble's only claim to fame was as the choice spot to shoot hare from the
"Rabbit" rail to Shreveport. The apricot nectar cake and Mandarin orange
cake float off the plate, and the southern pecan pie will give you an accent.

Tattletells now only opens for special functions of eight or more.
Showers, business dinners, and company functions can be held in the
"Adult Room," where the fireplace and the antique furniture make a group
of fifty seem intimate. The Adult Room also serves as the makeup room
during the frequent dress-up teas held in the smaller rooms next door. A
multitude of children's parties book these rooms with small fry dressed as
Scarlet O'Hara and little boys in top hats. They drink Tattletea and swap
elementary school war stories. Just because you are a big fry does not
mean you can't participate in an etiquette tea. You will no doubt have to
provide your own merit badge, though. The Girl Scouts enforce their age
limit.

House Tea: Oleta's Hot Spiced Tea

Hours: By reservation only

Location: First street is Highway 1960

Extended Services: Wedding and Baby Showers, Rehearsal Dinners, Receptions, Catering, Children's Dress-Up

La Porte

 The Two Sisters

101 E. Main Street
(Inside Antiques and Gifts by Parker)
281-470-0247

Although it is called Two Sisters, this tearoom could be more accurately described as Everyone in the Family tearoom. The two owners, Nan Brown and Betty Parker, enlisted the aid of their husbands and a myriad of family members to run this busy antique store and tearoom outside

Houston. At the end of the downtown strip, the Wedgwood blue building with the clean white porch railing and corner lattices is a welcoming sight in this sleepy bayside town.

Inside, the left side of the large room is dominated by antiques the owners have acquired. Betty shops for the vintage furniture and Nan acquires the glassware. The dark, glossy European desks and dining room tables are everywhere, smelling of history and lemon oil. Nautical and wartime memorabilia cover several surfaces. An 1841 English compass and binoculars sit next to an ancient sextant on a massive cherry wood partners desk.

The right side of the room is devoted to the tearoom. Encircled by a railing, the restaurant is designed to resemble a garden. The table linens are a mixture of soft pastels that match the walls and are easy on the eye.

For novelty, try eating in "The Bedroom" at the back of the store. The French doors lead to a table flanked by a heavy headboard. Various pieces of boudoir furniture complete the room. Where else can you get served lunch in bed?

House Tea: Rotates daily

Hours: (Store) Tues.-Sat. 10-5; (Lunch) Tues.-Sat. 11-3

Location: On Spencer Highway

Extended Services: Wedding and Baby Showers, Rehearsal Dinners, Receptions

Menu

Salads

Chicken Salad	Pasta Salad
Garden Salad	Tuna Salad

Sandwiches

Chicken Salad	Honey Ham and Cheddar
Smoked Turkey and Swiss	Pimento Cheese
Tuna	

League City

 ## Main Memories

3500 W. Main Street
281-554-2312

The town of League City has seen many types of farms since its days as a Karankawa Indian village. Since the 1890s, it has been home to a convict farm, a poor farm, a Humble Oil tank farm, many vegetable and fruit farms, and a notable egg farm. On FM 518 just outside of town resided the Hardy Egg Ranch, the first farm in the United States to house hens in coops. For many years the Hardy Egg Ranch ran a thriving business across vast acreage just inside the city limits. Today the ranch is the site of the Main Memories tearoom, "the best little teahouse in Texas."

The gravel driveway leads you up to the rustic house that was one of the original buildings. Inside, the tearoom has a ranch house feel. The wooden floors are well worn, and the living room is expansive. The wood beams vault across the ceiling and into the neighboring rooms. The chambers to the left are primarily for bridal parties and receptions. To the right is the main tearoom. Wooden tables are covered with woven throws, and the ceiling beams crisscross into stone walls. The effect is so much like dining at a dude ranch, you wouldn't be surprised to hear the dinner triangle clanging.

House Tea: Apricot

Hours: (Store) Tues.-Sat. 10-5; (Lunch) Tues.-Sat. 11-3

Location: Highway 518 on the fringes of the city

Extended Services: Wedding and Baby Showers, Rehearsal Dinners, Receptions, Catering, Cakes and Party Trays

Menu

Salads

Chef Salad - A variety of vegetables topped with turkey, ham, cheddar cheese, mozzarella cheese, and egg

Pasta Salad	Garden Salad
Chicken Salad	Tuna Salad

200

Sandwiches

Tuna Salad   Turkey, Ham, or Roast Beef
Hot Pastrami   Pimento Cheese

 South Shore Tearoom and Bistro

501 East Main #4
281-332-4069

When you are tired of the standard tearoom forage, it is time to take a short trip outside Houston and visit South Shore, where the entrees reflect the owner's native Louisiana heritage. Formerly known as "Her House and Pig Patch," this charming tearoom relocated to the little strip of Americana called Founders Square. Right across the street from the white gazebo of Founders Park and looking for all the world like a stage set for the movie *Pollyanna*, the converted houses are now eclectic retail stores.

Follow the white picket fence up to the white latticed front porch. You can park yourself at one of the tables here or step into the cool house. In the front room, the light reflects off the polished wooden floors from the row of oversized windows. A faux fireplace covers one wall, and café tables pepper the room. A miniature picnic table sits in the corner for the small fry. For more privacy, the Green Room in the back of the house overlooks the backyard through shuttered windows. Next to it, the Blue Ivy Room is divided by Japanese screens painted with teacups. This room also has a terrific view of the grassy lawn. If you are in the mood to perch, try a bar-stool or an overstuffed chair in the coffee bar. South Shore speaks both tea and coffee.

If it is Cajun food you are after, try their dinner menu, when the chicken salad gives way to gumbo and even the sandwiches acquire a kick. "Ah gay-ron-tee."

House Tea: Peach, Blackberry, or Mango in rotation

Hours: (Store) Mon.-Sat. 9-5, (Lunch) Mon.-Sat. 11-5

Location: In Founders Square at the corner of Park and Main

Extended Services: Wedding and Baby Showers, Rehearsal Dinners, Catering, Afternoon Tea, Coffee Bar

Menu

Salads

Grilled Chicken Salad - Tender grilled chicken served on a bed of lettuce garnished with cheese, egg, and tomato

Sandwiches

Turkey and Cheese   Ham and Cheese
Egg Salad   Tuna Salad
Chicken Salad   Cucumber Dill

French Dip - Beef served on a French baguette with cheese, lettuce, tomato, and au jus

Tearoom Club - Turkey, ham, cheese, and bacon

Grilled Chicken Sandwich - Grilled chicken breast, sliced tomato, spinach, and mozzarella cheese on sourdough bread

Entrees

Grilled Sausage - Italian sausage grilled, red and green bell pepper

Pork Chops - Grilled chops served with potatoes and vegetables

Grilled Rib-Eye - Served with vegetables and potatoes

Chicken and Vegetables - Grilled chicken breast sautéed, combined with broccoli, mushrooms, diced sun-dried tomato, and served with fettuccine pasta

The Unicorn

820 E. Main Street
281-557-0672

For years the wind has rustled the Spanish moss in the ancient oaks lining the streets of League City. The butter yellow Victorian house with the tin roof and wraparound porch continues to sit among its peers in the same old neighborhood, oblivious to nearby Houston growing up around it. Every bit as homey as it was to the original family who first lived there, this stately home is now the Unicorn.

Inside, the creaking wooden floors lead you to bright tailored rooms with white linens and gilt frames. The structure of the old house from the

tin roof to the polished pegged floor is original, and if you look closely, you can see the bubbles in the window glass that confirm their authenticity.

Owned by Nancy Lynn and David De La Rosa, the Unicorn is a family-run tribute to Nancy's mother, a woman of celebrated hospitality and grace. The members of the De La Rosa clan chip in their time, be it cooking, waiting, or chatting with you in the atrium. So welcoming are they, that neighbors who once lived in the surrounding houses often come to eat. Even one of the original owners of this house comes to visit on occasion. She likes to sit in the room that once was her master bedroom and reminisce about the rope swing out front. She says that it's the closest thing she gets to being served breakfast in bed.

House Tea: Green Tea with Mango

Hours: Mon.-Sat. 11-3

Location: Corner of Iowa and Main

Extended Services: Wedding and Baby Showers, Rehearsal Dinners, Dinner by Reservation only (Fri.-Sat.)

Menu

Salads

The Newcastle Garden Salad - A blend of garden greens garnished with tomato, cucumber, carrots, sliced green onion, and seasoned croutons

The Wakefield Chef Salad - Garden greens garnished with honey ham, smoked turkey, tomato, egg, cheese, and seasoned croutons

Sandwiches

The Duchess - A warm open-faced sandwich with turkey, ham, Swiss cheese, sliced pineapple, and a special herb sauce served on homemade honey oat bread

The Windsor - A warm open-faced sandwich with ham, Swiss cheese, broccoli spears, peach slices, and a creamy Parmesan cheese sauce

The Sheffield - An open-faced sandwich with tender slices of roast beef, Swiss cheese, cucumber slices, and a dill sauce

The Bismarck - Thin slices of smoked turkey breast, lettuce leaves, Swiss cheese, pineapple slices, and a creamy cranberry sauce served on a croissant

The Nottingham - The Unicorn chicken salad consisting of tender chunks of chicken mixed with sliced almonds, celery, green onion, and a creamy dressing

The Lancaster - The Unicorn shrimp salad consisting of delicate baby shrimp, green bell pepper, celery, green onion, and a creamy dressing with lettuce on a croissant

The King's Delight - Slices of corned beef topped with Swiss cheese, sauerkraut, and Thousand Island cream sauce

Entrees

The Balmoral - The Unicorn chicken salad stuffed in a tomato and served with cheese straws

The Cheshire Baked Potato - A baked potato topped with a sour cream herb sauce, cheese, and green onion

The Warwick Potato - A baked potato filled with honey ham, asparagus, and a hollandaise sauce

The Westchester Potato - A baked potato filled with smoked turkey, garlic butter, sour cream, and sliced green onion

Victorian Lady

404½ Houston
281-338-4472
http://www.ruscelli.com/thevictorianlady.htm

A fan across the lips meant "kiss me, you fool." A flower to the lips meant "you better believe it, baby," but petals pulled off and dropped on the floor meant "no way, loser." Victorian women were masters of silent communication. All of the social nuances were mandatory education for a young lady, as well as languages, manners, music, literature, and a list of other topics so extensive that very few contemporary men or women could compare.

At the Victorian Lady, avid historians J'Nean Henderson and Kim Sesher instruct fascinated guests on the intricate details of an 1800s curriculum. During Afternoon Teas in their refined drawing room or for group functions, ladies are taught to hold their cups with the spoons at a proper forty-five-degree angle, how to fold calling cards to denote special meanings, and how to dress like a proper Victorian lady. Teas can be accompanied by a fashion show with clothes ranging from the 1850s crinoline hoop skirts to the sleek Edwardian look of the 1900s. More than two dozen models—men, women, and children—demonstrate over 300 custom-made outfits. Skating, riding, and golfing habits are interspersed with the ball gowns, wedding dresses, and Civil War uniforms, and all are shown in chronological order.

The fashions are all contemporary constructions from authentic patterns. Each article is demonstrated as to proper wear and purpose. One particular demonstration is the dressing of a Victorian lady from the bloomers up. A model starts in the bloomers typical of the period. Layer upon layer is added: corset, stockings, hoop cages, crinolines, more crinolines, slips, underdress, overdress, cape, boots, and finally hat and gloves. The entire ensemble takes some time to don, and the need for a maid becomes apparent to most guests long before the dress finally goes on. Any swooning that occurs is usually from a guest contemplating wearing forty pounds of clothing and a corset in Houston in July.

Although the retro-clothes are undoubtedly alluring and definitely flattering, the demonstration will make you appreciate your Levis all the more. Let's give a big Victorian cheer for the invention of air conditioning.

House Tea: China Rose

Hours: Mon.-Fri. 10-3

Location: I-45, Exit 518

Extended Services: Wedding and Baby Showers, Tea Classes, Fashion Show

Missouri City

 Two Friends Tearoom

3340 FM 1092 Road

281-499-5412

You don't need to wait for the Snow Fest to visit Two Friends, but since there is usually about a snowball's chance in Houston of a white Christmas in Texas, why pass on the opportunity? Held in December, the Snow Fest in Missouri City offers a winter wonderland for kiddies of all ages, including those over twenty. Each year two huge snow cone machines pump out 100,000 pounds of the fluffy white alien stuff for the snowman creation laboratory and snowball fight battleground. Parades, live music, and other activities get you in the holiday spirit as well.

At any time of year, Two Friends Tearoom teems with activity. Inside the red brick building, the ornate British parlor setting draws crowds from around the area. Step through the dark green sitting room with its china display case and cherry wood furniture and make your way into the main dining area. Decorated in dark rose and white lace curtains and a delicate rose motif, the room flickers to the light of tiny lamps scattered strategically around the room. Bud vases with French roses compliment the floral table linens, and gild-framed pastoral scenes complete the English gentry look. A separate room stands by for larger groups, and the whimsical Adorable Friends room features a mural of the Mad Hatter's infamous tea party, complete with grinning Cheshire.

For a change of pace, try the tea sandwiches with soup plate. The combo includes little finger sandwiches, like pineapple with pecans and a wonderful spinach, sour cream, and water chestnut, and gives you just a tad of everything wonderful.

Stay tuned, Two Friends will soon offer romantic getaway dinners and tea tastings once a month to acquaint your taste buds with the finer leaves in life.

House Tea: Peach

Hours: Mon.-Sat. 11-2

Location: Highway 6 and Murphy Road in the Township Square

Extended Services: Wedding and Baby Showers, Rehearsal Dinners, Receptions, Tea Tastings

Menu

Salads

Caesar Salad - Romaine lettuce tossed with grated Parmesan cheese and a Caesar dressing

Chicken Salad - Chunks of chicken with homemade mayonnaise, celery, green onion, and walnuts

Spinach Salad - Chopped spinach, mushrooms, bacon, chopped egg, and a brown sugar wine vinegar dressing

Township Salad - Marinated strips of chicken, toasted almonds, and sesame seeds on a bed of Romaine lettuce, sprinkled with Parmesan cheese and vinaigrette dressing

Sandwiches

Chicken Salad Croissant
Spinach Salad Croissant
Egg Salad
Cucumber and Cream Cheese

Tuna Croissant
Smoked Turkey Croissant
Pimiento Cheese
Frisco Club Sandwich

Entrees

Ham and Broccoli Quiche - Diced ham, chopped broccoli, and sharp cheddar cheese

Nederland

¡◉¡ The Boston Tearoom

1204 Boston Avenue
409-722-9296

Every school child knows the story of the band of disgruntled colonists who decided to show the crown what they thought of the new tea tax by dumping boxes of the imports into the harbor. What you may not know is that long before the Brits decided that oolong was their cup of tea, Americans had been imbibing the heady brews left them by the Dutch in the 1660s. That same year, England imposed a tea tax that would lead to a century of smuggling by its own people, an opium trade with China, and the first blending of teas to accommodate the demand that had grown much greater than the supply. When the English added a heavy duty to the Americans, the colonists smuggled the leaves directly from Holland.

In December of 1773 the British East India Company, near bankrupt due to mismanagement, had seventeen million pounds of tea to hoist. The Parliament gave the company exclusive rights to the colonies, cutting out the American dealers entirely. The East India company thought the citizens of the colonies would appreciate paying less than the smugglers' prices, but the tea sold to them was stale, and they were taxed on it to boot. The women boycotted the shipment, but the captain had orders not to leave the port until the ships had been unloaded. After a meeting attended by 5,000 concerned citizens, fifty men dressed as Mohawk Indians dumped 342 chests of green tea valued at 10,000 pounds sterling into the frigid waters of Boston Harbor, creating the world's first iced tea. The king was not amused. Now you know the rest of the story.

The Boston Tearoom doesn't derive its name so much from that fateful rebellion as it does from the fact that it sits on Boston Avenue, but it's a sneaky way to inject trivia into the book. A stone's throw from Beaumont, the town of Nederland, Dutch for "lowland," boasts the ultimate place for parties and receptions. With a lovely Victorian carriage scene painted on the side of the building, the Tuscan style restaurant presents an elaborate setting in a most unlikely place. Chandeliers saved from historic ante-bellum homes suspend over the greenery-wrapped columns and brocade tables. The chairs, like the tables, morph from romantic pink to golden elegance depending on the special occasion. Fresh flowers always perch on the tables, and a waterfall cascades in the corner. The upstairs banquet rooms extend to ornate iron-railed balconies that overlook the cobblestone streets and Dickens-style street lamps of this Main Street city.

The menu changes with the parties, but a complimentary tea bread with cinnamon butter always warms up the taste buds. Crêpes top the specialties list along with the brownie truffle and the strawberry-coconut pecan decadence, whose recipe should be stolen if possible.

Even if you don't agree with the current state tax, kindly resist the temptation to reenact history. Boston's Raspberry tea should not be wasted on the fish.

House Tea: Raspberry

Hours: Tues.-Fri. 11-2

Location: Downtown

Extended Services: Wedding and Baby Showers, Rehearsal Dinners, Receptions, Catering, Children's Dress-Up, Afternoon Tea

Orange

Terrace Tearoom

11535 I-10 East
(Inside Interstate Antique Mall)
409-745-4999

The "Gateway City" of Orange once served as a stopping place for outlaws on their way over the Sabine River from Louisiana into Texas. In the 1920s the speakeasies and gambling halls like the Silver Slipper and Show Boat gave Orange a reputation that lasted for decades. Today it still serves the party crowd as the jumping off spot to the casinos of Shreveport and the watering holes of New Orleans. Busloads of would-be gambling millionaires unload at the Interstate Antique Mall for a little pre-slot shopping and a bite of lunch at the Terrace Tearoom.

True to its name, the Terrace Tearoom brings a little of the outdoors in. The French country style restaurant sports concrete floors painted with red bricks so realistic, you'll do a double take. The white wrought iron patio tables and chairs are situated around the deck, comfortably cushioned in florals and stripes. Red glass dishes and fresh flowers adorn every table. Fountains, shrubs, and potted trees complete the scene of the well-dressed backyard.

The lady of the house, Mary Silmon, creates all of the gourmet delights in the shop. The private recipe bread pudding compares in decadence only to the brownie dessert made with raspberry truffles, hot chocolate sauce, and ice cream. The specialty jams and jellies lining the shelves are available individually or in gift baskets. Before you leave, be sure to try their muscadine jelly. The berry comes from a vine that only grows locally.

House Tea: Raspberry

Hours: (Store) Mon.-Sun. 10-5:30; (Lunch) Tues.-Sat. 11-2

Location: I-10 Exit 869 on Southside

Extended Services: Wedding and Baby Showers, Rehearsal Dinners, Receptions, Catering, Children's Dress-Up

Menu

Salads

Chef Salad - Turkey, ham, lettuce, tomato, egg, and cheese

Chicken or Tuna - Pieces of tender chicken or tuna, celery, sweet pickles, apple, and pecans on a bed of lettuce

House Salad - Tossed greens, tomato, carrots, and cucumber

Sandwiches

Chicken or Tuna   Turkey Breast
Pimento Cheese

Pearland

 Four Friends

3816 E. Broadway
281-485-6484

Outside Houston, two sisters and their friends decided to proactively battle empty nest syndrome and open a tearoom together. They renovated
one of the oldest homes in the white blossomed city of Pearland and created a cozy, congenial bivouac for stressed Houstoners escaping the
terrors of interstate life.

All guests use the back door of the little white house like a neighbor.
The wooden floors lead you past handmade candles, trendy jewelry, and
collectible Victorian shoes in delicate fabrics, rhinestones, and ribbon
roses. The tearoom in dark burgundy and lace spreads across the front of
the house. A teapot border runs around the room behind the antique furniture. The rest of the decor changes daily as customers suddenly think of
places in their homes just begging for that "perfect piece."

Even though the nest didn't stay empty due to returning adult children
and new grandchildren, the four friends maintain the tearoom with the
same easy charm they've shown each other over fifteen years. It is due to

this atmosphere that Four Friends continues as the mainstay of showers, mother and daughter luncheons, and the occasional bunco gaming group. After lunch, if you are looking for reasons not to return to the city, visit the antique stores on either side of the tearoom and around the corner. You might find the perfect mirror to hang over that newly acquired "perfect piece."

House Tea: Hot Spice

Hours: Tues.-Sat. 11-3

Location: Highway 35 and FM 518

Extended Services: Wedding and Baby Showers, Rehearsal Dinners, Children's Dress-Up

Pear Tree

2306 North Main
281-485-1697

On the edges of Houston lies the town that began life as Mark Belt but today answers to Pearland due to the huge quantities of the fluffy white trees. Most of the original orchards of this "agricultural Eden" bit the sawdust during the Galveston hurricane of 1900, but fortunately for the town, another source of economy was soon discovered; oil that is, black gold, Texas tea. Recently, the namesake cultivar made its dramatic reentrance with a series of organized plantings by concerned "pear-ents," whose work around the courthouse is just now reaching fruition.

While you're admiring nature's handiwork, why not stop at the appropriately named Pear Tree Tearoom on Main Street. This 1800s feed store has been serving their singular pimento cheese between the Bartlett yellow walls for over thirty years. If you don't know what to order, grab a pear off the tree. The menu is printed on it. The Hot Spice tea serves as the specialty of the house. Customers start with a demitasse of the brisk brew before meals but often end up going home with a quart for dessert.

Pear Tree opens a couple hours early with a continental breakfast featuring muffins and, of course, fruit. Take a wild guess as to what type. That's right, cantaloupe.

House Tea: Hot Spice

Hours: Mon.-Fri. 9-2

Location: Highway 528 across from Pearland State Bank

Extended Services: Wedding and Baby Showers, Rehearsal Dinners, Catering

Taraiz's Gourmet

2401 S. Washington
281-485-7329

South of Houston stands the international house of Pearland, better known as Taraiz's Gourmet. Designated after the owner, Taraiz Karasa, whose given name was imported from France and surname migrated from Italy, this tearoom dishes up a touch of foreign intrigue in cleverly disguised country blue.

If you woke up this morning feeling Italian, the pesto, pastas, and Marsala on the chef's list will have you crooning arias. Say "oui" to the shrimp crêpes and quiche and "bonjour" to the Monte Cristo so fresh it just escaped from the Bastille this morning. For those with a Mediterranean bent, try the Greek salad with feta cheese and the super rich baklava. Or, if you want to dine closer to home, check out the chicken quesadillas or tortilla soup.

Of course, Taraiz's still serves standard tearoom favorites for chicken salad-o-philes. The real question remains, however, does the club croissant come from Turkey or from Hamburg?

213

House Tea: Apple Cinnamon

Hours: Tues.-Fri. 11-2

Location: Washington and Highway 518

Extended Services: Wedding and Baby Showers, Rehearsal Dinners, Receptions, Catering, Afternoon Tea

Menu

Salads

Fresh Fruit	Spinach Salad
Garden Salad	Chef's Salad
Grilled Breast of Chicken Salad	Greek Salad
Caesar Salad	Caesar Salad with Chicken

Sandwiches

Chicken Salad Supreme	Ham and Turkey Club Croissant
Tuna Crunch	Classic Pimento Cheese
Monte Cristo	Sante Fe Sandwich

Richmond

 Sandy McGees

314 Morton Street
281-344-9393

On the perimeter of Houston, the sister cities of Richmond and Rosenberg share a secret: They both possess a Sandy McGees tearoom. Originally started fourteen years ago in the little house in Rosenberg, Sandy's became known for its fine food and beautiful presentation among the cheerful, multicolored rooms. Currently the house operates primarily as the catering headquarters but still offers the same extensive menu as the Richmond location.

In Richmond a turn-of-the-century mercantile houses the tearoom as well as the original soda fountain the owner frequented as a girl. Perch on one of the authentic stools and grab one of the best malts around or move

through the French doors to the terrace tearoom in the back. The Garden Room, with its twenty-foot ceilings, muraled walls, white linens, and tea lights gives way to the whimsical Parlor Room. Dressed in McKinsey style, black and white check tablecloths with bright splashes of accent colors, the Parlor is a visual overload of flashing pink flowers, busy pottery, and luminescent tearoom paraphernalia. In the corner, a wicker loveseat with throw pillows and coffee tables await the next Afternoon Tea, which is served in lavish style.

Sandy's menu offers a large range of soup, salad, and sandwich choices for the very hungry. Be sure to try the broccoli cheese soup, made and consumed in thirty-gallon batches daily. Buy a bowl or a gallon for late night noshing.

If you get the chance, wander around the tearoom and look at the paintings. Some of them depict a local artist's view of the ghost attorney that is said to haunt the back staircase. You can fill in your own lawyer joke punch line here.

The historic town of Richmond supposedly hosts a few spirits of its own. Looking around the antiquated downtown that plays the backdrop in films at least once a month, you can easily understand why the name of Richmond frequently appears in poltergeist stories. Take in the rustic buildings, old signs, and streetlights, and you might spot a familiar landmark one day in a favorite flick.

House Tea: Gold Rush Tea

Hours: (Lunch) Mon.-Fri. 10-5, Sat. 10-3; (Tea) Mon.-Sat. 4-6

Location: 4th and Morton. One block from Highway 90

Extended Services: Wedding and Baby Showers, Rehearsal Dinners, Receptions, Catering, Children's Dress-Up, Afternoon Tea

Menu

Salads

Pasta Salad - Tri-color pasta with vegetables, cheese, and a creamy Italian dressing

Spinach Salad - Spinach leaves with bacon, mushrooms, purple onion, Swiss and Parmesan cheese tossed with honey mustard dressing

Garden Salad - Leaf and iceberg lettuce, tomato, green pepper, carrots, radishes, mushrooms, and cheese served with buttermilk ranch or no fat raspberry vinaigrette

Chef's Salad - A garden salad with lean turkey and ham

Chicken Salad   Chicken Salad in Avocado or Tomato

Sandwiches

Chicken Salad - Chicken breast with celery, pickles, and lemon zest

6th Street Sandwich - Turkey or ham with avocado slices, alfalfa sprouts, baby Swiss and cheddar cheese, spinach leaves, lettuce, and tomato

Max Out Sandwich - Turkey sandwich with melted Swiss cheese and topped with a spinach salad

Po Boy - French bread with ham, turkey, salami, baby Swiss, cheddar, lettuce, tomato, mayonnaise, and chow chow

French Dip - Medium rare sirloin roast served in French bread with au jus

Club Croissant - Croissant with turkey bacon, Swiss, lettuce, and tomato

Grilled Chicken - Served with avocado and Swiss cheese

Entrees

Stuffed Spud - Baked potato with butter, sour cream, green onion, cheddar cheese, and bacon

Sante Fe Spud - Baked potato with butter, pico de gallo, cheddar cheese, grilled chicken breast, avocado slices, and chives with Albuquerque ranch dressing

Rosenberg

 Sandy McGees

1207 6th Street
281-341-9151

(See Sandy McGees - Richmond)

House Tea: Gold Rush Tea

Hours: Mon.-Fri. 11-2

Location: 6th and Avenue J

Extended Services: Wedding and Baby Showers, Rehearsal Dinners, Receptions, Catering, Children's Dress-Up, Afternoon Tea

Spring

 The British Trading Post

26303 Hardy Street
281-350-5854

For the true atmosphere of England from food to service, none matches the British Trading Post. Spanning one end of Spring's artsy Old Town circle, the Trading Post adds an authentic European touch to the art galleries and specialty shops of this ski village look-alike town. The Union Jack proudly flies over the white front porch, proclaiming its independence from Southern Charm and the Spirit of the Old West Stores nearby.

The interior exudes the Brit feel as well. The dark green entryway sports flying pheasants, and the sunny porch with the green and white tablecloths are surrounded by photographs of Lady Diana and Queen Elizabeth. The Trading Post menu also speaks with an English accent. Steak pies with mushy peas are offered along with specialties that include Trifle, Crab Diane, Shrimp Sarah, and Breast of Chicken Victoria.

Thomas Garway's Coffee House in London was the first to publicly sell tea.

The Trading Post serves an elegant four-course Afternoon Tea on Royal Daulton china with scones and savories. Because, one should never "trifle" with Afternoon Tea.

House Tea: Black Current

Hours: Tues.-Sat. 11-3

Location: Farthest end of Old Town Circle

Extended Services: Wedding and Baby Showers, Rehearsal Dinners, Catering, Afternoon Tea

Menu

Sandwiches

Ham and Cheese   Open Faced Albacore Tuna
Chicken Salad

Entrees

Breast of Chicken Victoria   Quiche of the Day
Crab Diane   Shrimp Sarah
Shrimp Alexander   Meat Pie of the Day
Pastie of the Day   Sausage Rolls and English Beans

 The Garden Tearoom

16646 Champion Forest Dr.
281-251-1151

When was the last time you went to a restaurant where the people truly enjoyed working there? Think hard, there'll be a ten-point quiz later. When's the last time you weren't introduced to the hostess as Mr. and Mrs. Non-Smoking? Here's the big money question. When's the last time that a waiter *didn't* look like he or she was mentally web surfing while reciting the specials for the day? "Dude, that's KingRanch @Chicken.com."

At the Garden Tearoom in Spring, the owner and staff so enjoy what they do that the customers frequently remark on the novelty. Owner Sherrie Holan considers the tearoom a gift. One day while trudging through the slog that was her former job, Sherrie decided to step out on faith and quit to find a happier pursuit. Very shortly afterward, while conversing with a woman next to her at a Bible study class, she discovered that the lady was searching for a new owner for her tearoom. Sherrie snatched it up and everyday thereafter can be seen dancing to work, carrying fresh flowers from her garden to adorn the antique lavender and lace tables.

Inside the tearoom, wisteria and ivy drape from the ceilings. Lace curtains hang in the windows, and a piano waits patiently in the corner. Feel free to do your Liberace impression, or keep your day job and listen to the professional pianist, who plays once a week. If it seems a shame to dine inside on such a beautiful day, slurp your poblano pepper soup on the patio tables in the front. Indoors or out, you'll be smiling before the Chocolate Eruption Mousse cheesecake appears at your table.

House Tea: Raspberry, Tropical Paradise, or Passion Fruit in rotation

Hours: Mon.-Sat. 11-3, Fri. 5-8

Location: At Champion Forest and Louetta (in Randall's Center)

Extended Services: Wedding and Baby Showers, Rehearsal Dinners, Receptions, Catering, Children's Dress-Up, Afternoon Tea

Menu

Salads

Cobb Salad - Chicken, tomatoes, bleu cheese, bacon, and avocado with mixed greens and Brown Derby dressing

Cathy's Pasta - Pasta, basil, garden vegetables, chicken, and sunflower seeds with a Brown Derby dressing

Cobbler Salad - Spinach greens, Greek olives, feta cheese, red bell pepper, and bacon in a creamy garlic dressing

Peppered Popcorn Chicken - Fried bite-size chicken served over mixed greens with cheddar and Monterey Jack cheeses

Avocado Boat - Chicken or tuna salad served in an avocado half with mixed greens and cucumber slices

Sandwiches

The BLT - Bacon, lettuce, and tomato

The Veggie - Slices of avocado, tomato, cucumber, green pepper, lettuce, and alfalfa sprouts in a secret sauce

Chicken Salad - Seasoned baked chicken breast in a basil and Parmesan dressing with tomato and lettuce

Garden Club - Slices of turkey breast, lettuce, tomato, cucumber, green pepper, bacon, onion, and honey mustard

Callie's Ham and Cheese - Slices of ham, Muenster cheese, and a secret sauce in a croissant

The Garden Deli - Ham or turkey stacked on choice of bread with lettuce, tomato, and cheese

Tropical Chicken Wrap - Roasted chicken, Muenster cheese, lettuce with toasted almonds and tropical sauce in a flour tortilla

Turkey Peso Wrap - Oven roasted turkey, homemade pesto spread, lettuce, tomato, and alfalfa sprouts in a flour tortilla

Tuna Salad - Albacore tuna, pineapple, walnuts, sweet relish, and purple onion

Entrees

Monday = Chicken crêpes with broccoli and cheddar cheese

Tuesday = Linguini with Maria's meatballs

Wednesday = Shrimp fettuccine

Thursday = King Ranch chicken

Friday = Baked fish in white wine sauce

Saturday = Chicken Cordon Bleu with American cheeses and mushrooms

Quiche of the Day

 Queen Victoria's English Tearoom

310 Main Street
281-288-7455

Near the Wild Goose Chase, the Pampered Princess, and the Potbellied Cricket, the dark maroon house of Queen Victoria's Tearoom lures tired shoppers for a quiet lunch. Good Queen Vicky would have liked this dim tearoom with the forest green velvet drapes. Flower vases, and a hodgepodge of antique napkin rings sit atop three-tiered table linens in maroon and green. Over the cozy two-tops, photographs of the majesty herself preside with an upstart teenager named Elizabeth. Queen Victoria's makes excellent quiche, including broccoli-mushroom and southwest, but most locals return for the special recipe chicken salad.

While you are in town, check out some of the great stores in Old Town Spring, like the Memory Depot for the A to Z of scrapbooking, the Little Dutch Girl for all things Hollandish, or the Old Texas Woodcarvers Shop for hand-carved dogwood jewelry. If you get done early, bypass the fudge and return to Queen V's for some of their fresh blackberry or peach cobbler. It's thoroughly decadent.

House Tea: Raspberry, Blackberry, or Honey Lemon in rotation
Hours: Tues.-Sat. 11-3
Location: Old Town Spring on left side of loop
Extended Services: None at this time

Menu

Salads

Shrimp Salad in Whole Stuffed Tomato - Gulf shrimp in a tomato
Chicken Salad - Chicken breast with walnuts and a dash of curry
Seafood Salad - Shrimp and crab

Sandwiches

Ham and Cheese   Turkey
Chicken Salad   Seafood Salad

Entrees

Ham and Cheese Quiche   Spinach Quiche
Southwest Quiche   Broccoli Mushroom Quiche

The Rose Teacup

315 Gentry Street #1A
281-353-5566

In darling Old Town Spring, if you cannot find the perfect present for everyone you know, sort of know, and want to know, you aren't looking very hard. The downtown circle overflows with galleries, specialty shops, and antique stores lining the brick streets of this 1900s railroad town and opening onto bustling alleys. Depression era glass shines in one window while canary yellow and hot pink skirts flutter in the breeze outside a boutique. Newcomers crisscross the streets like kids in Beanie Babyland, buying Chinese koi kites, banana nut candles, Amish hex signs, and authentic bosun's whistles.

In the center of the controlled chaos, the pink and lace oasis of the Rose Teacup extends a delicate cup of Guava Peach to passersby. Enter the frosted oval front door and set your shopping bags down next to the lace table skirts. A china cabinet with cups, saucers, and gourmet coffees covers one wall, and a faux fireplace faces a garden mural at the back of the room. The menu at the Rose Teacup changes slightly with the seasons. During the hot summer months, cool soups like celery almondine are served instead of the hearty jalapeño potato or zucchini brown rice stews served in winter.

> Darjeeling, Lapsang Souchong, and Gunpowder tea should never be mixed with milk.

A Place In Time adjoins the tearoom, and the owners, Mary Ann and Troy Smith, take turns running both businesses. The store carries Tiffany-style lamps, Russian teapots, pink porcelain chocolate pots from the Czech Republic, and antique furniture small enough for toting back to the big cities.

If the weather feels too glorious to stay indoors, you can have your tea and crumpets on the patio. Pecan trees shade the cobblestone courtyard, and cool breezes trickle through the alleys. It's a people-watching heaven.

House Tea: Guava Peach or Strawberry Apricot Papaya

Hours: Mon.-Sun. 11-5

Location: Gentry Square in Old Town

Extended Services: Wedding and Baby Showers, Rehearsal Dinners, Children's Dress-Up, Afternoon Tea

Teddi's Restaurant and Tearoom

9001 Louetta Road
281-251-5055

One of the most frequented meeting grounds in Spring is Teddi's at the corner of Louetta and Champion. Walking up to the front door, you get a chance to admire the artistry of the floor-to-ceiling glass windows that surround the building. The paintings depict garden scenes with thatched cottages and the ubiquitous hollyhocks in a style reminiscent of Thomas Kinkade paintings.

Inside the bright, uncluttered restaurant, you may choose whichever room matches your mood. The Teapot Room with its crisp pale blue and white stripes, tailored table linens, and recessed shelves reminds the visitor of a Mary Poppin's era breakfast nook. If you get the chance, take a look at the collection of teapots on the back wall. Diners in the Garden Room bask in the rays of sunlight streaming through the long windows. Accented in purple wisteria and dark green ivy, this room attracts the outdoorsy crowd. Of the three, the frilly mauve Victorian Room with its crystal chandeliers seems to be the most popular.

As a drag racing enthusiast, owner Teddi regrets not having time to get to the racetrack as often as she'd like. The lunch, dinner, and Afternoon Tea the restaurant serves keep her perpetually busy. She still shows support for her favorite Nascar team by treating Dave Marcos (#71) and crew to a big vat of crawfish, shrimp, and crab when they hit town. His autographed picture hangs in a place of honor in the front entryway.

Teddi's is booked yearly for many functions including showers, rehearsal dinners, and business meetings. It is also home to the "We're Not Martha Stewart" party, in which everyone brings their worst craft ideas. Popsicle stick chandeliers, lampshades made of marbles, and cat-hair oven mitts are all toted to the tearoom where they get extra points for humor and pointlessness. Participants are accepted even if they can't turn a dried turkey bone into a catalytic converter.

House Tea: Apricot

Hours: Mon.-Sun. 11-3; Mon.-Thurs. 5-9; Fri., Sat. 5-10; (Tea) Mon.-Wed., Sat. 3-5

Location: At the corner of Champion Road

Extended Services: Wedding and Baby Showers, Rehearsal Dinners, Catering, Afternoon Tea

Menu

Salads

Teddi's Waldorf Chicken Salad - Chunks of chicken breast, red delicious apples, celery, and walnuts blended with a creamy dressing on a bed of greens

Tuna Salad - White meat tuna, hard-cooked eggs, and celery blended with dressing and served on a bed of greens

Shrimp Salad - Gulf shrimp blended with egg, celery, and creamy herb dressing on a bed of greens, garnished with slices of tomato, hard-cooked eggs, and avocado

Fruit Salad - Creamy molded fruit salad surrounded by seasonal fruit with a burgundy poppy seed dressing or a reduced fat honey poppy seed yogurt dressing

Grilled Chicken Caesar Salad - Romaine, toasted croutons, and grilled chicken breast served with Caesar dressing

Sandwiches

Smoked Turkey Salad - Smoked turkey, hard-cooked eggs, and chopped spinach blended with a creamy herb dressing

Bill's Original - Slices of chicken breast and provolone cheese topped with a coconut almond dressing and garnished with greens

Ole Fashioned Hamburger - Grilled lean ground beef, tomato, lettuce, and onion served on a toasted seeded roll

Reuben Sandwich - Sliced lean corned beef, sauerkraut, Swiss cheese, Thousand Island dressing layered between two slices of seeded rye bread and grilled

California BLT - Bacon, lettuce, tomato, sprouts, and avocado

Virginia Baked Ham - Virginia baked ham, Swiss cheese, and lettuce topped with honey mustard dressing

Waldorf Chicken Salad Sandwich - Chunks of chicken breast, red delicious apples, celery, and walnuts blended with a creamy dressing

Best of the Wurst - Liverwurst, tomato, and purple onion served on rye bread and topped with choice of mayonnaise or horseradish mustard

Tuna Salad - White meat tuna, hard-cooked eggs, and celery salad

Egg Salad - Hard-cooked eggs, green olives, and a dab of horseradish blended with mayonnaise

Stuffed Pita Pocket - Mushrooms, carrots, cucumber, avocado, and Swiss cheese

Entrees

Chicken Fettuccine Alfredo - Chicken breast topped with green and white fettuccine and Parmesan cheese sauce

Chicken Tetrazzini - Creamy blend of spaghetti, cheese, chicken breast, and mushrooms

Pasta Primavera - Steamed vegetables, pasta, and a pesto sauce

Teddi's Quiche   Baked Potato

Tomball

 Whistle Stop

107 Commerce
(Inside Relics by the Railroad)
281-255-2455

Just outside of Houston and a few miles from the permanent Renaissance Fair in Magnolia lies the oil town of Tomball. Named for Thomas Henry Ball, the attorney responsible for routing the railroad line through the town, this settlement found a new life when oil was discovered in its baseball field in 1912. The Humble Oil company, now called Exxon, set up shop and encouraged population growth by giving the residents free gas until very recently. This flourishing city is now home to Compaq Computers.

Near the spot of the old depot, the aptly named Relics by the Railroad offers antiques and gifts stores along raised walkways. Overlooking a recessed garden, the Whistle Stop Tearoom booms with business inside the vibrant yellow and navy walls. Strictly unfrilly, this tearoom serves its Royal Cup tea in pilsner glasses and its sandwiches on huge slabs of bread baked every morning by two local Czech families. Although known for its bread pudding made from fresh croissants, the dessert case at the front of the store will stop you in your tracks. The real cream on the chocolate fudge cream pie is three inches thick and is surely made with four cans of

Eagle Brand milk. The chocolate layer cake has the old-fashioned kind of fudge icing, and the piña colada cake is as light as a feather. If you cannot finish it all, not to worry. That is why poodle pouches were invented.

House Tea: Passion Fruit and Red Raspberry

Hours: Mon.-Sat. 11-3

Location: Behind Main Street at Walnut

Extended Services: Wedding and Baby Showers, Rehearsal Dinners, Receptions, Children's Dress-Up

Menu

Salads

House Salad - A blend of European greens, tomato, cucumber, and sprouts

Spinach Salad - Baby spinach with bacon, mushrooms, sprouts, and toasted almonds

Chicken Salad - A scoop of chicken salad with herb dressing on a bed of lettuce surrounded by pasta salad and topped with sprouts

Chef Salad - Ham and turkey breast spirals with veggies and cheese on a bed of European greens

Sandwiches

Chicken Salad - Creamy blend of white chicken with herb dressing and topped with lettuce and sprouts

Jalapeño Pimento Cheese - Mix of two cheeses, pimentos, and spicy jalapeños

Ham and Cheese - Honey ham with Swiss cheese, lettuce, mustard, and mayonnaise

Turkey - A stack of sliced turkey breast with Swiss cheese, lettuce, mustard, and mayonnaise

Tuna Salad - Made with tomato, cucumbers, spinach, lettuce, and sprouts with Swiss cheese, mustard, and mayonnaise

"Great love affairs start with
champagne and end with tisane."

– Honore De Balzac

South/Gulf Coast

Drinking to Antiquing—What to Do with Those Tea Leaves

For thousands of years, people of the western world have stared into their pots in dismay. Oh, what to do with those soggy little leaves once the brew is happily imbibed? Great poets suggested a solution:

The tea was lovely, dark and deep,
but I have promises to keep,
and leaves to burn before I sleep.

Philosophers added their voice:

I drink therefore I am... stumped.

Even artists considered the problem. Many people don't know that Rodin's *Thinker* is actually contemplating how to get to the compost heap and back wearing his birthday suit without getting arrested.

The Chinese sprinkled their Gunpowder Green over the Szechwan and chowed down... wallah, problem solved. Meanwhile, the rest of the world watched and waited. Today we women of the naught-ies (the years following the nineties) have a cornucopia of options passed to us by wise ancestors and fertile contemporary minds. Choose your favorite method of disposal. However, you may want to wait to try these *after* you've left the tearoom.

- Soak your tired tootsies in a cool, Peppermint bath.

- Apply used Green or Black tea bags to puffy eyes. Make sure you don't use Cranberry tea or you may have eyes redder than you started with.

- Throw Green or Chamomile tea in your bathwater for a super-relaxing soak.
- Dye those annoying gray hairs with Black tea or boost your henna's color variation.
- Soak objects in strong tea to give them that antique look. Black tea converts underwear into a chic-khaki fashion statement.
- Black tea and witch hazel make a good skin toner. Pep your tan and open those pores.
- Clean your counters. The acidity in tea cuts right through grease. Better not use it on white counters, though.
- Say *bon voyage* to fleas. Sprinkle dried leaves on your carpet, on your dog, or both and then vacuum the carpet. No need to vacuum the dog. The fleas will hop the first train out of town. They must be coffee drinkers.
- Enhance your potting soil. Plants love old, used tea leaves.
- Bite on a wet tea bag to kill teething pain, canker sores, or dental abuse.
- Make potpourri from your favorite blend.
- Boil those old tea leaves in pans to remove intractable smells.
- Slap a wet tea bag on an insect bite, inoculation, or other skin scrape. It pulls the sting. Try Peppermint tea on your sunburn. Ah, sweet relief.
- Tea in the refrigerator absorbs stinky food odors.
- Cold, used tea bags clean glass and mirrors quite effectively.
- Drink it. This is probably the best use for tea ever invented.

Bay City

 Lagniappe

2125 Avenue G
979-244-3538

In French, lagniappe means "a little something extra," and that describes Joan Dickerson's gift shop to a "tea." For six years the shop has presented unusual collectibles and home accessories to the folks of Bay City. The interior design background of Joan's daughter comes in handy when selecting the lamps, rugs, and mirrors for the chic crowd, but true to its name, Lagniappe offers several little extras. Old World Christmas collections fill one corner next to the trendy Jeep Collins jewelry, made by hand in the Hill Country. One entire section is devoted to Christopher Radko ornaments, which tend to be a hot commodity long after the holidays.

When the turn-of-the-century lawyer's office became vacant next door, Joan expanded service to include a tearoom. The distressed tiles and wall paint scraped down to the multishaded bottom layers give Lagniappe an eccentric hacienda appeal. No boring wooden chairs for this place. Check out the wild stainless steel chairs with backs made from old teaspoons. Interior designers find all the best stuff.

House Tea: Raspberry

Hours: (Store) Mon.-Fri. 10-5:30, Sat. 10-5; (Lunch) Mon.-Sat. 11-2

Location: Highway 35

Extended Services: Wedding and Baby Showers, Rehearsal Dinners, Afternoon Tea

Brazoria

 French Doors

907 N. Highway 36
979-798-0885

After years of arguing about the name of their annual celebration, the people of Brazoria finally compromised. So this year make plans to visit the No Name Festival held just outside the 42,000 coastal acres of the Brazoria National Park. Over 250 species including snow geese, mottled ducks, and gala attendees enjoy this wildlife refuge. When you are ready to soak up the remnants of your bacchanalia, look for the six black portals of the aptly named French Doors Tearoom.

> The first crop of Darjeeling appears in April and has a light, fragrant taste. The main crop comes in the second flush and has a fruity flavor.

Overlooking Highway 36, the restored 1920s house with its ten-foot ceilings dishes out some hefty helpings of bayou booty. Owned by Devonna Thompson, a second generation Louisiana-ite, French Doors peppers its menu with spicy snacks, like Cajun tuna, jalapeño potato soup, and boudin balls, which combines rice and sausage in perfect croquette harmony. More modern than frilly, the ivory linens and dishes along with the stemmed goblets jazz up the teal and black tables and gold walls. Simple Easter lilies in elegant vases add that *Architectural Digest* touch. If you need an airing, take your tea at the bistro table on the front porch. You can wave at the commuters like one of the "beautiful people."

House Tea: Earl Grey

Hours: Mon.-Fri. 11-2

Location: Corner of Brooks (Highway 36) and Pleasant

Extended Services: Wedding and Baby Showers, Rehearsal Dinners, Catering, Afternoon Tea

Brownsville

 Palm Court

2200 Boca Chica Boulevard
956-542-3575

Every winter Brownsville becomes the home for snowbirds of both avian and human persuasion. Only a few miles from the herons and rare brown pelicans of Port Isabel and the bird sanctuaries of South Padre Island, Brownsville lies in the flight path of many migratory species. Over the years it has claimed its place as the premier bird watching area in Texas. After a day of watching pelicans fish, doubtlessly you will be ready to feed your own gullet. Travel to the ultra vogue Palm Court for some shrimp rémoulade and cocoa mocha pie.

Nestled among Country Casuals clothing store and Second Thought home accessories, Palm Court serves its repast in style. An enormous crystal chandelier dangles thirty feet in the air and sparkles in the paladin windows and mirrored French doors. The white latticed walls match the refined ivory linens, and every table comes adorned in orchids specially imported from Costa Rica and displayed in long-stemmed crystal vases.

The menu packs a few pleasant surprises, including gazpacho, chicken crêpes, and Better Than Sex pie, which comes with a pecan crust; cream cheese, chocolate, and vanilla filling; almonds; and whipped cream.

If you haven't tired of observing the animal kingdom, visit the extraordinary Gladys Porter Zoo, a thirty-one-acre open-air preserve of endangered species, separated by moats, caves, and streams instead of cages.

House Tea: Spice Tea

Hours: (Store) Mon.-Sat. 10-8; (Lunch) Mon.-Sat. 11-3

Location: Two blocks from Expressway 77/83

Extended Services: Wedding and Baby Showers, Rehearsal Dinners, Receptions, Weddings

Menu

Salads

Chicken Caesar Salad - Romaine lettuce, slices of chicken breast, tomato, and croutons tossed in a Caesar dressing

Spinach Salad - Leaf spinach with bacon, toasted croutons, and hard-boiled eggs

Shrimp Rémoulade - Shrimp tossed in a rémoulade dressing served on an avocado half

Chicken Salad or Tuna Salad - Served on a bed of lettuce and garnished with tomato and eggs

Sandwiches

The Executive Sandwich - Lean ham, tender roast beef, breast of turkey, and Swiss cheese on pumpernickel bread

Turkey Huntington - Lean breast of turkey layered with cheese, alfalfa sprouts, and avocado topped with buttermilk dressing

French Dip - Slices of roast beef, sweet onions, Swiss cheese, and horseradish sauce served on a French roll

Entrees

Lasagna Primavera - Noodles layered with beef, vegetables, ricotta cheese, and mozzarella cheese topped with marinara sauce

Herb Chicken - A boneless breast of chicken stuffed with a blend of herbs and cream cheese topped with a white wine sauce

Chicken-Broccoli Casserole - Diced breast of chicken and broccoli in a mild curry and cheddar cheese sauce

Chicken Crêpes - Topped with a mushroom and herb sauce

Quiche Florentine - Baked with bacon and cheese in a flaky crust

Meat Loaf Florentine - Meat loaf filled with spinach, mushrooms, and pearl onions

Ceylon, a leading tea producer, started growing the shrubs when a blight wiped out the coffee plantations.

Corpus Christi

 Jeron's Tearoom

517 Everhart
(Inside Sister Sue's Antiques and Uniques)
361-980-1939

For 300 years Corpus Christi existed as just one more landlocked bay on the Texas coast. Since the Army Corps of Engineers dredged the ship channel in the 1920s, the city has boomed with military traffic and melanoma-seeking snowbirds armed with Budweiser towels and Panama hats. For these adventurers, Corpus offers something for everyone.

At the aquarium you can pet stingrays and see who made the "Jellyfish of the Month" honor roll. Watching those little scorpions-of-the-sea performing water aerobics to New Age jazz is hypnotizing but still won't cause you to run right out to the pet store for one of your very own. At night the USS *Lexington* glows the ghostly blue of its Japanese nickname. After a day of claustrophobic touring, you can lie on the beach and watch the Daisy Scouts skunk the Cub Scouts on the lateral gun cranks. For sheer entertainment value, nothing matches the Officer on Deck shouting boot camp orders to wide-eyed toddlers amidst parental snickers. In the marina, moored among the sleak indulgences, float full-scale replicas of the leaky, creaky tubs Columbus used to cross the ocean blue. Picturing eighty-seven men packed into those tiny, rat infested, aquatic coffins for eight months makes you wonder how America was ever discovered again, again. For the sentimental, who could bypass the bronze statue of Selena on the pier? Sea air does make you thirsty, however, and fortunately Jeron's is poised right around the corner inside Sister Sue's Antiques and Uniques.

Dressed in white linen, cream, and eggplant, Jeron's is an "island of serenity in a chaotic world." Study groups, new neighbor associations, and bridge clubs make this tearoom their second home. They come for the meetings but return for the quiche, which remains the uncontested specialty.

Now you can stop by Jeron's on the way to Mexico. Carnival Cruise Lines recently added Corpus as a departure port for Jamaica, Cozumel, and the Grand Caymans. *Olé!*

House Tea: Lemon Blossom and Wild Raspberry

Hours: (Store) Mon.-Sat. 10-6; (Lunch) Mon.-Sat. 11-2

Location: Everhart and Alameda

Extended Services: Wedding and Baby Showers, Rehearsal Dinners, Catering, Afternoon Tea

Freeport

 Picket Fence

831 W. 2nd Street

979-233-4135

(See Picket Fence - Lake Jackson)

House Tea: Peach, Tahitian Breeze, and Red Raspberry

Hours: Mon.-Fri. 11-2

Location: Valasco and 2nd

Extended Services: Wedding and Baby Showers, Rehearsal Dinners, Children's Dress-Up, Afternoon Tea

Gruene

 The River House Tearoom

1617 New Braunfels

830-608-0690

Rising from the river far below, the shouts and laughter of parboiled tubers floating down the Guadalupe reach your ears. Under the cool shade of the ancient oaks, you sip iced tea and compliment yourself on your choice of primo locations. Just a splash up the river from New Braunfels, historic Gruene straddles the Guadalupe and serves as an onramp for convoys of college rafters undertaking a three-hour scenic suntan, cooler in tow. This charming 1870s German township doesn't just appeal to students. A roundabout of specialty shops housed in the original homes and mercantiles offer pottery, jewelry, and rustic artwork. On warm summer evenings, the country music pours out of Gruene Hall, Texas's oldest kicker barn and the launchpad of stardom for Lyle Lovett, George Strait, and Hal Ketchum. On the deck of the Gristmill Bar, tourists sit above the

original river-powered cotton gin that processed Gruene's number one cash crop and watch the sunset and masochists-in-motion.

Around the corner, you sit on the forest patio of the River House Tearoom. Next to you the Queen Anne gingerbread house with blue and maroon piping attracts a bustling business of hopeless romantics who adore the European china, silver dessert goblets, and hand-painted teapots among the country floral decor. But the patio tables are the best seats in town. You can split the artichoke stuffed with goat cheese with someone you love so you'll have plenty of room for the coconut shrimp in orange champagne sauce. The diverse gourmet menu contains heavier choices that make this a restaurant in tearoom disguise, but certainly appealing to almost every taste. At the River House Tearoom you can fulfill at least two points of Gruene's motto: Eat, shop, sleep, drink, float. You can accomplish the other three on your way out of town.

House Tea: Rotates daily

Hours: Tues.-Sun. 11-4

Location: Exit 191 off I-35

Extended Services: Wedding and Baby Showers, Rehearsal Dinners, Receptions, Catering, Afternoon Tea

The courthouse was built to end the bickering and remains on the National Register of Historic Places. At Christmas the lights suspended from all four corners of the bell tower have illuminated the streets of this historic town every year since 1938, darkening only during World War II.

House Tea: Orange Dreamsicle and Raspberry Passion

Hours: Tues.-Thurs. 11-1

Location: South side of downtown square

Extended Services: Wedding and Baby Showers, Rehearsal Dinners, Receptions, Weddings

Lake Jackson

 ## Apple's Way

145 Oyster Creek Drive #6

979-297-0072

Fifteen minutes from the coast, the city of Lake Jackson spins an interesting tale of its inception. Originally, Dow Chemical Company bought the 3,000-acre sugar and cotton plantation owned by Major Abner Jackson to convert to a townsite for their employees. The land included the surrounding water: Lake Jackson, Lake Flagg, and two unnamed lakes. Alden B. Dow and J. P. Dunbar designed the town enshrouded in parks and horseshoe-curved streets named after trees and flowers. Both men must have been closet tree-huggers because this gulf city, cloaked in massive live oaks, receives the Tree USA award year after year. Encircling the town lies Wilderness Park, the vast undeveloped area extending to the Brazos that Dow maintains in its natural state as a wildlife preserve.

Lemon tea should never be served in Styrofoam cups. The acid in the lemon causes the polystyrene to dissolve into the tea.

In keeping with the arbor theme, Apple's Way Tearoom celebrates the owner's tree of choice. Granny Smiths dance on the wallpaper around the Washington blue and white rooms. One of the house specialties remains, of course, apple dumplings, although the cheese broccoli soup and pizza quiche get the most encores. No matter which dish you order, it comes complete with a Macintosh wedge to cleanse the palate. Bill Gates would be scandalized.

House Tea: Orange Pekoe

Hours: Mon.-Sat. 11-2

Location: Highway 288 and Oyster Creek Drive

Extended Services: Wedding and Baby Showers, Rehearsal Dinners, Catering

Picket Fence

708 Dixie Drive
979-297-7234

Only in Lake Jackson could directions sound like an Abbott and Costello routine.

"Which way to the store?"

"Any Way."

Just remember that although This Way, That Way, and Any Way are street names, the church resides on His Way, and One Way is a smart idea. It's not that the residents of the town attempt to confuse tourists, but that most folks in Lake Jackson have lived there since heck was a pup and already know how to get around.

The Picket Fence Tearoom of Lake Jackson is the first of two tearooms bearing that name. The original restaurant became so successful that the neighboring city of Freeport established another equally as popular. True to its name, white picket fences decked in flowers and birdhouses adorn the shelves, rafters, and spare corners of the room. The hand-painted tables carry individual themes. The ABC table sports the letters of the alphabet, the Rose and Birdhouse tables face the one painted with Noah's ark. Even the chairs hold bold, colorful seat cushions.

If you get the chance, visit during the annual Mosquito Festival held in honor of the "Texas state bird." It's the most fun you can legally have with an insect.

House Tea: Peach, Tahitian Breeze, and Red Raspberry

Hours: Mon.-Sat. 11-2

Location: Highway 332 and Dixie Drive

Extended Services: Wedding and Baby Showers, Rehearsal Dinners, Children's Dress-Up, Afternoon Tea

San Antonio

 Apple Annie's

555 W. Bitters Road
210-491-0226

In 1878 Baron George von Tomasini, an Austrian immigrant, left his wife and kids in the homeland to pursue his fortune in Mexico. He returned in glory only to find his wife had presumed him dead and remarried. So, the Baron journeyed to Texas to get hitched anew and build a life on the 400 acres he bought in rural San Antonio. On that property now stands the houses of several of his descendants, Artisan's Alley, and the estates of Hill Country Village, which are so big that their garage and bathroom have separate zip codes.

In a style reminiscent of the former Ola Podrida Mall in Dallas, Artisan's Alley collects upscale boutique shops and sets them in rambling corridors of wood beams, sharp turns, and pleasant surprises. Past the fluffy chenille robes in the Homebodies Sleepwear shop and the stuffed bears dressed like Teddy Roosevelt, past camp shirts with smiling cats in Ray Bans, and next to the tapestry table runners of the English Ivy interiors store, Apple Annie's Tearoom fills the terraced rooms at the back of the building.

Multiple rooms of red and white checked tables with matching ruby napkins and chair cushions accommodate the volume of visitors. A spacious porch overlooks the yard two stories below through window bookshelves bearing apples and other knickknacks. Several rooms cluster around the bakery counter, sweetly torturing the customers with the siren song of chocolate. If the weather is fair, the patio tables with red and white umbrellas sunbathe just outside the porch doors. From that vantage point, you can watch people run up and down the stairs to the birdhouse store above and munch on your ham and cream cheese on toasted raisin bread. It's a tough job, but somebody's got to do it.

House Tea: Peach and Raspberry

Hours: (Store) Mon.-Sat. 10-6, Sun. 12-6; (Lunch) Mon.-Fri. 11-2:30, Sat. 11-3, Sun. 11-3, desserts served until 5

Location: At Bitters and Blanco Road

Extended Services: Wedding and Baby Showers, Rehearsal Dinners, Receptions, Catering, Weddings, Cooking Classes

Menu

Salads

Chicken Salad	Tuna Salad
Chef Salad	Chicken Taco Salad

Sandwiches

Chicken Salad - Breast of chicken and seasonings

Tuna Salad - Albacore tuna with chopped apples

Breast of Turkey - Thin sliced turkey breast and lettuce

Roast Beef - Choice round, lettuce, and tomato

Grilled Ham and Swiss - Thin slices of ham and Swiss cheese, lettuce, and tomato on rye

Hawaiian Ham and Pineapple - Thin slices of ham, cream cheese, and pineapple spread on raisin toast

Club Sandwich - Bacon, tomato, lettuce, and ham or turkey with American or Swiss cheese

Vegetarian - Three cheeses, black olives, onion, tomato, lettuce, and choice of dressing

Egg Salad - Served on white, wheat, or rye

BLT - Bacon, lettuce, and tomato

Monterey Open Face - Monterey Jack, ham, lettuce, tomato, avocado, and bacon on rye

Epicurean Sandwich - Hot, open-faced sandwich on toasted wheat with turkey breast, ham, sautéed mushrooms, cheddar cheese, and white wine sauce

Old-Fashioned Reuben - Grilled corned beef on dark rye bread, Thousand Island dressing, and melted Swiss cheese

Cold California Chicken Wrap - Served with avocado, tomato, onion, Monterey Jack, and peppercorn ranch dressing

Entrees

Quiche of the Day   Pasta du Jour

 The Carriage House

555 Funston
210-821-6447

At the Carriage House in San Antonio, you can fulfill your lifelong desire to have tea in a horse stall. But what a horse stall! Heavy oak doors trimmed in dark green and wrought iron swing open to the terra-cotta tiles, oiled wooden tables, creamy limestone walls, and the white linens of the restored Sullivan carriage house. Originally built as the stables and Model T parking lot for cattle king Daniel J. Sullivan, the building was meticulously disassembled from its home on 4th and Broadway. Stonemasons marked each limestone block and reassembled the giant jigsaw puzzle in the Botanical Gardens, where it became a gift shop, lecture hall, and tearoom.

The Carriage House serves gourmet specialties from the mind of Chef Ed Vervais. Pimento cheese sandwiches come with a dab of cranberry spread. Walnuts and Mandarin oranges complete the chicken salad, and all meals are blessed with dark, sweet raisin bread. Never have your daily oats tasted so good.

House Tea: Raspberry

Hours: Tues.-Sun. 11-2

Location: In the Botanical Gardens

Extended Services: Wedding and Baby Showers, Rehearsal Dinners

 ## Fancy That!

18770 Nacogdoches Road (FM 2252)
210-651-9716

The jets of nearby Randolph Air Force Base rumble over the old farmhouse of Fancy That! Tearoom, and the ladies of the staff jostle each other to wait on the flyboys who visit for lunch. Originally, Elizabeth Boyer spotted the dilapidated turn-of-the-century barn and house lounging in a twelve-acre forest at San Antonio's city limit. She fell in love with the

> In France milk was added before the tea to protect the porcelain cups from shattering.

buildings and coerced her family to undertake the miraculous transformation from decrepit to adorable. Now, a rose of Sharon drapes over the trellis leading into the front yard. On the left, a whimsical wrought iron flower "bed" overflows with colorful pansies. Up the wooden porch and past the white wicker furniture, the lovely house with cheery rooms of ice cream

parlor chairs and wooden tables seems to agree with its new life as a tea-room. A variety of cozy rooms empty off the main entrance, but the enclosed back porch that overlooks the bird feeders and forest is the most enchanting. For those of us who don't know a scissortail from a blue jay, the owners kindly posted a bird identification chart on the wall, and all through lunch occasional exclamations of "Oh look, a goldfinch!" inter-rupts the chicken salad.

Next door, the distressed wood antique barn has gained a fame of its own as a backdrop on several record albums. The double-story loft interior provides space for the antique sideboards, cradles, and wardrobe cabinets sold. Outside, a Railway Express Agency train wagon awaits your luggage, and Texas-shaped flagstones walk you to your car. Such a surprise to have a bit of the countryside in the middle of a sprawling metropolis...Fancy That!

House Tea: Wild Berry, Peach, or Cinnamon Apple (changes with season)

Hours: Mon.-Thurs. 10-6, Fri.-Sat. 10-8

Location: Two miles north of Loop 1604

Extended Services: Wedding and Baby Showers, Rehearsal Dinners, Receptions, Children's Dress-Up, Afternoon Tea

Gini's Restaurant and Bakery

7214 Blanco Road
210-342-2768

But Lancelot mused a little space;
He said, "She has a lovely face;
God in his mercy lend her grace,
The Lady of Shalott."

Tennyson may have never visited Gini's Restaurant and Bakery, but many other British poets have. In spring when Austin holds its annual poetry festival, Gini's hosts the immensely popular British Poetry Benefit Lunch. For several hours, contestants from the Old World mesmerize guests with recitals of famous and new works while sipping their extra dark, extra hot Assam. According to the poets, Gini's is the only place to get "real" tea in the colonies.

Originally, Gini Crowley ran a health food store and juice bar, which she converted into a Pritikin fare café. Over the years, she continued to add to the eclectic natural foods menu until the restaurant served an eight-page variety of vegetarian home cooking in the "upscale sixties hippie ambiance." Eventually, Gini's English boarding school upbringing asserted itself, and she built an old-fashioned tearoom inside the original restaurant. Among the twelve-foot *Alice in Wonderland* murals, customers sip traditional English teas on French porcelain with pink linens. Each place setting contains a waste bowl, which refined tea drinkers use to dump their cold tea before receiving a refill.

Before you hit the road, you may want to grab some munchables from the bakery. Their specialties include Victorian sponge cake, cranberry-orange scones, and homemade Scottish shortbread.

House Tea: Whittard's Assam

Hours: Mon.-Sat. 8-8, Sun. 9-2

Location: Lockhill-Selma and Blanco

Extended Services: Wedding and Baby Showers, Rehearsal Dinners, Receptions, Catering, Afternoon Tea, Wedding Cakes

Menu

Salads

Popeye's Delight - Spinach leaves with mushrooms, red onion, egg, alfalfa sprouts, and sesame seeds

Greek Salad - Feta cheese, tomato, green peppers, and Greek olives piled atop greens

Caesar - Traditional Caesar salad topped with choice of avocado, grilled chicken breast, or tuna salad and topped with croutons, a tomato wedge, and Parmesan cheese

Mt. St. Helen - A mountain of greens with Monterey Jack or low-fat cheese, avocado, tomato wedges, egg, mushrooms, alfalfa sprouts, sesame and sunflower seeds

Sorry Charlie - A sea of greens topped with water-packed tuna salad, egg, tomato wedges, avocado, mushrooms, alfalfa sprouts, raw sunflower and sesame seeds

Grilled Chicken Salad - Salad mix topped with grilled marinated chicken breast, tomato wedges, avocado, alfalfa sprouts, and sesame seeds

Big Vegetarian Salad - Romaine, leaf, and iceberg lettuce, spinach, sliced carrots, yellow squash, red cabbage, avocado, tomato, mushrooms, alfalfa sprouts, sesame and sunflower seeds

Sandwiches

Honeybaked Turkey Breast - Thinly sliced honey baked turkey breast with green leaf lettuce and tomato on toasted wheatberry

Meatloaf - On wheatberry with lettuce and tomato

Deluxe Club - A double-decker on toasted wheatberry with turkey, ham, Swiss cheese, bacon or avocado, leaf lettuce, and tomato

Grilled Cheese and Tomato - Grilled Monterey Jack and grilled tomato slices on wheatberry bread

Cream Cheese and Cucumber - Thinly sliced cucumber and low-fat cream cheese on whole wheat

Deaf Smith Peanut Butter, Honey, and Banana - Sun roasted peanut butter on whole wheat or wheatberry

Turkey Meatball Submarine - Low-fat turkey meatballs served on French bread

Turkey, Ham, and Swiss - Thinly sliced turkey, ham, and low-fat Swiss cheese on toasted wheatberry

King Avocado - Sliced avocado, thinly sliced mushrooms, melted Monterey Jack, lettuce, tomato, alfalfa sprouts, sesame seeds, and sunflowers seeds on toasted wheatberry

Tuna Salad - Water-packed tuna salad with finely chopped carrots, celery, sweet pickle relish, egg, mayonnaise, and lemon juice on toasted wheatberry with lettuce, tomato, and alfalfa sprouts

Madhatters

3606 Avenue B
210-821-6555
http://www.madhatterstea.com

Madhatters of San Antonio definitely gets the award for most avant-garde tearoom in Texas. With hours extending till 10 P.M., you can "sip under the stars" on the gravel patio surrounded by *Alice in Wonderland* signs that read "up," "down," "this way," and "right way." They even found a perfect use for that old barbecue grill. Turn it into a petunia planter. The funky fifties and sixties à la Austin bistro look seems right at home in the theater strip behind Brackenridge Park. Don't confuse Madhatters with a

coffeehouse, they only serve one type of the dreaded bean for die-hards, but they serve over forty-three loose teas, including Spring Cherry, Tea of Inquiry, Blackberry Sage, and an entire series of superior estate teas. Now is your chance to see if you have the palate of a blue blood.

Madhatters serves formal teas as well as a wide variety from a menu that reads like a who's who in Lewis Carroll books. For breakfast, try the Try Me, Have Me, Eat Me breakfast burritos or the Woofles, which are inverted waffles. Alice's Adventurous Sandwiches and the Rabbit's Big, Big Salads win the day with tea-smoked chicken as an option. No matter what you order, you have to check out the psychedelic tostada chips in canary yellow, cobalt blue, fire engine red, and M&M green. They'll blow your mind. This is absolutely the spot to bring guests from New York.

House Tea: Blackberry, Unleaded, and Peach in rotation with forty other varieties

Hours: Mon.-Fri. 7:30-10 P.M., Sat. 10 A.M.-11 P.M., Sun. 9-9

Location: Tuleta and Avenue B behind Brackenridge Park

Extended Services: Wedding and Baby Showers, Rehearsal Dinners, Catering, Breakfast, Dinner

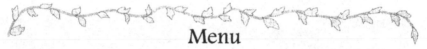

Menu

Salads

Mediterranean Tea Smoked Chicken over Organic Field Greens - With black olives, sun dried tomato, onion, cucumber, feta, oregano, and a tea vinaigrette

Grilled Turkey over Organic Field Greens - With roasted pecans, avocado, pickled onion, tomato, cucumber, feta, boiled egg, and a tea vinaigrette

Tea Smoked Chicken over Organic Field Greens - With roasted pecans, avocado, pickled onion, tomato, cucumber, feta, and a tea vinaigrette

Tea Smoked Chicken Caesar of Organic Field Greens - Traditional dressing with eggs and anchovies

Chipotle Tuna Salad Plate - Over field greens with avocado, cucumber, tomato, blue corn chips, pickled onion, and a tea vinaigrette

Spinach and Chicken Salad Plate - Over field greens with cucumber, tomato, blue corn chips, pickled onion, and a tea vinaigrette

Mixed Field Greens - With roasted pecans, avocado, pickled onion, boiled egg, feta cheese, cucumber, tomato, and a tea vinaigrette

Sandwiches

Cucumber, Cream Cheese, and Avocado   Fabulous Veggie
Spinach and Chicken Salad   Smoked Salmon
Smoked Jalapeño Tuna Salad   Queen of Clubs
Grilled Southwest Reuben   Grilled Three Cheese
Grilled Spinach and Chicken Salad   Turkey and Pepper Jack Melt
Imagine Your Own Sandwich

Turkey, Avocado, and Chipotle Cream Cheese

Mini Mansions

8407 Broadway
210-826-4223

Grab a book from Viva Books next door and plunk down at one of the tables in Mini Mansions. The tearoom that shares its deck space with a gallery and bookstore seems the perfect place to enjoy a quiet read in the filtered

sunlight. On the left side of the Connecticut-boardwalk style strip, the tea-room began as a natural extension of owner Margi Groos's catering business. Folks can enjoy her specialty dishes in the quiet coffeehouse environment. White tables with pink umbrellas are scattered over the distressed wood decking leading into the cool interior. Inside, local art traded with the art gallery next door brightens the walls while ceiling fans spin overhead. The dark oak tables and chairs give the restaurant a comfortable, university dive look.

Margi's catering menu lists an intriguing blend of the unusual and southern favorites, including apricot Brie in puff pastry with grapes, grilled orange pork tenderloin, and whipped sweet potatoes. Some of the dishes are featured as specials along with the standard light fare menu and comfort food daily specials, like King Ranch chicken. When you've finished your book, you have just enough time to catch an art lecture at the gallery. Just look around the tearoom's walls if you want to know what the topic is.

House Tea: Mint Lemon

Hours: Mon.-Sat. 11-2

Location: Greenbrier and Broadway at Highway 410

Extended Services: Wedding and Baby Showers, Rehearsal Dinners, Catering

Menu

Salads

Garden Salad   Grilled Chicken Salad
Tuna Salad   Chicken Salad

Sandwiches

Chicken Salad   Tuna Salad
Ham and Cheese Croissant   Pimento Cheese
Egg Salad

Entrees

Artichoke Quiche   Chicken and Broccoli Quiche
Ham Quiche   Quiche Lorraine
Spanish Quiche   Spinach Quiche
Tomato Eggplant Quiche

Scrivener's

8502 Broadway
210-824-2353

Time to build that addition to your home, so you'd best wander down to the tearoom for two by fours. While you're at it, grab some grass seed and cinnamon rolls. Scrivener's is certainly the last word in one-stop shopping. When Cousin Ernie started his lumberyard in the pastures of post-World War II San Antonio, people generally regarded him as two tacos short of a fiesta dinner. But Ernie continued to add section upon section until the business became the something-for-everyone emporium that exists today.

To get to the tearoom, you must enter the hardware store

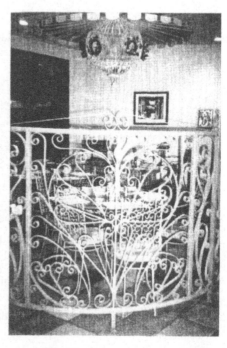

and walk past the nails and sprinklers in the shape of tractors. Through the archway, you wander past the china and crystal shop, then the card and party supply store. Hang a left at the fabric, and you can see the tearoom just past the clothing boutique. A mint green fence in wrought iron filigree corrals the leisurely placed glass and iron tables. Matching chairs with floral cushions perch on the terra-cotta tiles.

Multiple generations of the Scrivener clan have run the tearoom over the years, and many of the recipes have been handed down through the family. The secret of the shrimp salad originated forty years ago along with the bouillon, which is made the old-fashioned French way with veggies and herbs boiled then strained to retain the elusive essence of Southern garden. The cinnamon rolls remain the signature dish, and the owners will tell you "they're the best in the world. That's not Texas bragging. It's just a fact." Apparently the customers agree because a multitude of nods from around the restaurant respond to this statement. Grab some to go, and you're ready to finish that addition to your house.

House Tea: Orange Pekoe

Hours: Mon.-Sat. 11:30-3:30

Location: Loop 410 and Broadway

Extended Services: Wedding and Baby Showers, Rehearsal Dinners, Hardware, Fabrics, Lumber

Menu

Salads

Shrimp Salad   Chicken Salad
Tuna Salad   Cobb Salad

Sandwiches

Sliced Chicken   Chicken Salad
Baked Ham   Tuna Salad
Bacon, Lettuce, and Tomato   Pimento Cheese

Entrees

Shrimp Florence - A large tomato stuffed with boiled shrimp, garnished with cucumber, avocado, hard-boiled egg, and rémoulade dressing

Chicken Crêpes   Enchilada Plate

San Marcos

 ## The Tearoom

4200 IH-35 South
(Inside Gregson's Antiques)
512-392-5696

On the way to tubing on the Guadalupe or to pick up those Air Jordans, drop by The Tearoom in San Marcos for the freshest provender in town. Across the highway from the Tanger Outlet Mall, The Tearoom attracts its share of Liz Claiborne aficionados, Levi-aholics, and Reebok junkies trying to recharge their batteries before re-charging their credit cards.

To the rear of the Gregson Antique Mall, past the Harvard Science Lab cabinet and other fabulous vintage furniture, The Tearoom reclines across the back of the building, separating its diners from the hustle and bustle of enthused antique collectors. The mahogany buffets, sideboards, and china cabinets around the room are all for sale as well as the prints framed by the owner himself. Miniature teapots with daisies and ivy adorn the floral tables with their green checkered skirts and country wooden chairs.

Joyce Kidd, the co-owner, makes everything from the chicken salad to the baked flounder from scratch when you order them, but the freshness is well worth the slight delay. While you wait, try the freshly squeezed cherry lemonade. It'll give you the energy you need to attempt more structural damage to your checking account.

House Tea: Peach, Strawberry, and Raspberry

Hours: Mon.-Fri. 11:30-4:30, Sat.-Sun. 11-6

Location: Across from the outlet mall

Extended Services: Wedding and Baby Showers, Rehearsal Dinners, Catering, Afternoon Tea

Menu

Salads

Fresh Garden Salad   Fruit Salad
Spinach Salad

Sandwiches

Tuna Salad
Chicken Salad   Turkey or Ham on a Kaiser Roll
Roast Beef and Cheese on a Kaiser Roll
Pimento Cheese on Toasted Whole Wheat

Schertz

 Bawdsey Manor Tearoom

124 Schertz Parkway
210-659-8766

So lovely to see you at Bawdsey Manor! On the petticoats of San Antonio, this British grocery, gift shop, and English tearoom satisfies all of your mushy pea needs and crispy chip cravings. As you walk into the dim interior, you are instantly surrounded by the controlled clutter of an English emporium. Even if your larder needs no restocking, it's fascinating to scope out the supply of Brit indispensables. Shelves of shepherd's pie mix

nudge cans of Shipman's wholesome sar-
dine and tomato, pronounced to-mah-to,
spread. Bangers, kippers, and creamed rice
enjoy their place in the spotlight next to
microwaveable treacle in golden syrup,
which the manufacturer touts as "naughtily
nostalgic." You can even buy decaf Ty-phoo,
whatever that is.

> Tea should be kept in a
> dry, light-proof
> container, like a tin
> can. If tea gets wet you
> can cook it in the oven
> on a cookie sheet.

Past the drygoods, the cozy Conserva-
tory and Maypole rooms seat a gaggle of small, mismatched tables.
Despite the lace and teapot decor, Bawdsey exudes a rustic charm, which
probably explains the fifty-fifty balance in clientele. Grab a *Union Jack*
newspaper from the rack and find a seat if you can. Word of mouth keeps
Bawdsey mobbed for lunch, Afternoon Tea, and Friday night's fish and
chips. If the thought of more chicken salad makes you cluck, you will be
delighted by their meat pies and mash, or shepherd's pie, the recipe for
which was reputedly given "by the shepherd himself." On your way out,
don't forget to help yourself to a miniature Union Jack flag at the counter.
Waving it might even help you remember all the lyrics to "Rule Britannia."
You get ten points for every word you know after "Britannia all the way."

House Tea: P. G. Tips

Hours: (Store) Tues.-Thurs. 11-4, Fri. 11-8, Sat. 1-5; (Lunch) Tues.-Thurs. 11-3, Fri. 11-8, Sat. 11-4

Location: Schertz Parkway and Highway 78

Extended Services: Wedding and Baby Showers, Rehearsal Dinners, Receptions, Afternoon Tea

Sweeny

 ## Patty Cakes

304 N. Main
(Inside My Cousin's Place)
979-548-1234

At My Cousin's Place, the owners have that his and her thing down to a fine art. Seated deep in the heart of Phillips Petroleum country, the restaurant serves buffet lunch and dinner to hungry plant workers. Owners Julie Heinrich and Shirley "as in Temple" McKee wanted a place for the ladies to call their own. So, they built Patty Cakes Tearoom inside the other restaurant, and the two businesses coexist peacefully with the gift shop to arbitrate. The tearoom is a pastel contrast to the dark greens of Cousin's Place. The piano hiding among the potted plants, bookshelves, and flowers promotes impromptu recitals among the elderly ladies. Each visitor receives a cup of Cinnamon Orange Spice tea and a Patty Cake from the great-grandmother's recipe. The only item on the menu set in proverbial stone is Wednesday's delectable tomato basil soup. Customers discover the menu selection when they receive the weekly fax blast. Save room, the homemade apple strudel will make you yodel.

> Tea drunk after a meal with a high fat content will help the body digest faster.

House Tea: Cinnamon Orange Spice

Hours: (Restaurant) Mon.-Sun. 6:30 A.M.-2 P.M., Mon.-Fri. 5 P.M.-8:30 P.M.; (Tearoom) Mon.-Wed. 11-1:30

Location: Downtown

Extended Services: Wedding and Baby Showers, Rehearsal Dinners, Catering

West Columbia

The Feed Store

333 West Brazos
979-345-6997

West Columbia, the real first capital of the Republic of Texas, has been home to many celebrated individuals. Sam Houston was inaugurated on the steps of the capital in 1836, and Stephen F. Austin lived and died here. Governor James Hogg and his daughter, Ima, owned a plantation off Route 35 that now covers sixty-six acres. Even Carrie Nation, the violent prohibition activist, owned a hotel here that remained untouched by the city fire of 1889. She considered this an indication that she was born divine. Historic markers pepper the roadsides and buildings of West Columbia and provide enlightenment into the political world of the 1800s.

To complete your historic pilgrimage, visit the Feed Store for some gourmet vittles in the country ambiance. This 1938 building operated as a feed store until the Junes converted it into a tearoom. The cream and army green checked walls, wood floors, and tin panels are original. None of the architecture of the building has been modified. Even the handmade bricks dug from slave ditches can still be seen in the interior columns. The decor of the tearoom echoes the country feel

> Between the 1900s and World War II, tea dances in England allowed unescorted woman to meet the gentlemen of their dreams to the strains of a full orchestra.

of the architecture. Green and cream checked and floral tablecloths cover the rustic furniture.

Along with a standard menu, the Feed Store serves a hot entree combination that changes daily and a tomato basil consommé apéritif with a cucumber sandwich-ette. If you are a tea taster, try the locally processed Kevton teas. The Feed Store serves and sells a wide variety, including Black Currant and Peach Apricot.

House Tea: Peach Apricot and Black Currant

Hours: (Store) Tues.-Sat. 10-6; (Lunch) Tues.-Sat. 11-2

Location: Across from the new post office

Extended Services: Wedding and Baby Showers, Rehearsal Dinners, Children's Dress-Up

Sweet P's Eatery

409 W. Brazos
979-345-4330

"Blessed when you come in and blessed when you go out," reads the version of scripture over the archway in Sweet P's Eatery. Literally housed in an adorable 1927 home, Sweet P's feels like a trip to Grandma's place. When owner Pam Sparks bought the property from the last surviving child of the original family, she had the gypsum board stripped to reveal textured wooden walls to match the oak and pine floors. Pam planted the garden with roses in the same hues as the celadon green, pink, and burgundy of the interior, and a white picket fence was added so visitors could find the house hidden from the main road. With the familiar cooking smells wafting from the kitchen and the soft instrumental music barely audible over the drone of busy bees in the garden, the peacefulness of this tearoom lulls you into a post-lunch daydream of dozing in a hammock, one of Grandma's oatmeal cookies clutched in hand. As appealing as that prospect sounds, the San Jacinto festival comes but once a year and you'll not want to miss it.

Apart from the carnival and other kiddie attractions, the Varner Hogg Plantation celebrates the Battle of San Jacinto with a live display of weavers, blacksmiths, and candle makers plying their trades. Militiamen in period uniforms camp under the Spanish moss and perform drills during the day. If you haven't filled your hunger for history, the West Columbia museum displays a wealth of regional artifacts, including slavery implements.

House Tea: Peach

Hours: Mon.-Fri. 11-2

Location: Next to the power company. Look for the picket fence.

Extended Services: Wedding and Baby Showers, Rehearsal Dinners, Catering

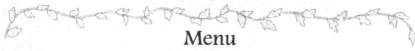

Menu

Salads

Chef Salad - Meat, cheese, and boiled egg on a bed of greens

Sandwiches

Grilled Reuben on Rye - Corned beef, Swiss cheese, Thousand Island dressing, and sauerkraut served on grilled rye

Turkey or Ham Croissant - A croissant with choice of sliced turkey or ham, mayonnaise, lettuce, and tomato

Grilled Chicken Pita - Honey pita bread with grilled chicken, lettuce, tomato, and cheese served with ranch dressing

Muffaletta - Round Italian specialty bread with ham, salami, two different cheeses, and an olive relish dressing

Hero - Ham, salami, Muenster and provolone cheese on a hoagie bun with mayonnaise and mustard topped with lettuce and tomato

Honorable Mention - Hico

 Wiseman House Chocolates

Rt. 2, Box 173
254-796-2565

In the newly created category of "Places We Wish Were a Tearoom," special honors go to Wiseman House Chocolates in the Old West town of Hico. Parked at the intersection of Highway 281 and Highway 6, the lovely, Queen Anne style home was built for F. Rufus Wiseman, a famous portrait photographer, and his bride, Adeline. Now, newlyweds LaDonne and Kevin Wenzel fill the squeaky wooden floors with eccentric art, clever gifts, and most especially chocolate par excellence. For the strict tea-goer, try the Earl Grey or Green Tea truffles, made like all of the cocoa masterpieces in the Switz tradition. For you femme fatales, and you know who you are, the decadent Wicked Woman dark chocolate truffles await you.

Although the darling house fairly begs for a tearoom and the Wenzels admit they've thought seriously about opening one, none exists as of yet. So, when you are tooling up Highway 281, drop by and convince Kevin that his life would not be complete without this addition. For incentive, just think of the desserts they could offer: cappuccino milk chocolate truffle brownies with a raspberry sauce, apricot cream truffle pie, or white chocolate truffle mousse with fresh strawberries. Chocolate lovers of the world, unite!

House Tea: Republic of Tea all varieties

Hours: Mon.-Sat. 10-6, Sun. 1-5

Location: Highway 281 and Highway 6 "at the only blinking light in town"

Extended Services: Gifts and Chocolate Shop

Author's Note: In the process of writing this book I tried in earnest to find every tearoom that wanted to be found, but some of you hide better than the others. If somehow I missed you, please let me know for inclusion in possible future editions.

Danke Mucho,

Lori Torrance
QA Chicken Salad Dept.
lori_torrance@yahoo.com

Index

I

J

K

L

M

Y

Z

Made in the USA
Coppell, TX
29 March 2022